RUNNIN
THE DEVIL

Essays, Articles and Remembrances

John Albert

Punk ★ Hostage ★ Press

RUNNING WITH THE DEVIL

Essays, Articles and Remembrances

ISBN: 978-1-940213-28-6

Editor
Joe Donnelly

Foreword
Ben Harper

Cover Photo
Jennifer Finch

Cover Design
Julia Kwong

PUNK HOSTAGE PRESS
Hollywood, California
www.punkhostagepress.com

For Ravi

"It is the soundtrack to a world that doesn't exist anymore. I know because that world is where I come from."

— John Albert

Table of Contents

Introduction

By Joe Donnelly

John Albert's final words for me were about heading off towards a certain death. They came in the form of a text he sent me a few hours before he died in the early morning of May 3, 2023, at the age of 58. The text was a short video clip from *Encounters at the End of the World*, Werner Herzog's Oscar-nominated 2007 film documenting the stark beauty of Antarctica and the intriguing creatures who live and work there.

Some of them are penguins, including the doomed star of the sequence John sent me. The clip features a penguin who refuses to return with his compadres to the relative safety and comfort of their oceanside rookery following the brutal brooding season, during which male penguins stand upright and cover their eggs with their warm pouches for 65 days, enduring the harshest conditions the planet can offer. Instead of going home, this penguin marches off towards the mountains and the frozen, foodless interior. This happens often enough, with outcomes inevitable enough, that Herzog advises viewers in his frank and wrenching manner that when it comes to these "disoriented or deranged" penguins, *"the rules for the humans are, do not disturb or hold up the penguin. Stand still and let him go on his way. And here, he's heading off into the interior of the vast continent. With 5,000 kilometers ahead of him, he's heading towards certain death."*

It's fitting that Herzog's voice in my ear would be John's parting gift to me. We loved Werner for all his deadpan lust for life and keen awareness of death. It's also fitting that I didn't get the text until the morning after John had sent it to me, when I was sitting on the toilet digesting the news that my friend had been taken by a heart attack in the wee hours. Heart sagging, mind reeling, nature calling, I scrolled through my messages and up popped John from the beyond, hitting me with the full weight of Herzogian existentialism while I took a crap. Anyone who knew John, knows he was looking down at this scene with absurdist glee.

It runs the risk of being too Didionesque to search for meaning in the coincidence of John sending me that text just hours before he died. Moreover, John would frown upon me for doing so: we both regarded Joan Didion's unifying theories, particularly those attempting to illustrate a prevailing ethos, with a bit of skepticism. Still, as the lady said, we tell ourselves stories in order to live. Or, like Herzog in his Antarctic documentary, and John in his writing, to try to make sense of life in the face of certain death.

John was highly attuned to the ephemeral nature of life, and any meaning we might ascribe to it, perhaps because so many of his friends preceded him to an early death. I don't think it's any coincidence that the exurban malaise depicted in Didion's SoCal dystopia, "Some Dreamers of the Golden Dream," inhabits the same smoggy eastern edges of Los Angeles where John and his latchkey cohorts came of age between the tailwinds of hippie idealism and the headwinds of Reagan-era self-centeredness. This was John's milieu, a fertile time and place for fledgling critical thinkers, especially precocious ones such as John. He would channel his ferocious precocity in various ways: as a brazen dissident, a juvenile-delinquent junkie, a death-rock pioneer, and, finally, as a closet intellectual (as he put it) who uniquely articulated the forces that shaped him and his contemporaries.

What were those forces? Didion might describe them as an itchy restlessness stirred by the Santa Ana winds and the edge of the desert. John wasn't nearly as deterministic. He preferred to call a void a void. Or, as he wrote it in "The Satori Underground" from the anthology *Yes Is The Answer*:

> *For some inexplicable reason, my friends and I wanted desperately to be old and jaded. For me, the oppressive stillness of the Southern California suburbs and an inner emotional turmoil resulted in a painful restlessness. For others, including Dwight, there were also broken homes. All this merged with above average intellects to create a hunger for adventure which drew us to new music and literature, but also a destructive underworld of drugs and crime. And so instead of skateboarding and kissing girls we spent our teenage years using heroin and dressing like middle-aged criminals from some dreary, nonexistent European city of another era.*

John, an exceptionally charismatic person, cofounded Christian Death, played drums with Bad Religion, and influenced many notable figures in the Los Angeles underground of the 80s and 90s. As he got sober and older, he would be known widely for his wit, withering or puerile as the occasion demanded, as well as his love of baseball, dogs, and surfing. He became a loyal friend to many and dedicated father to his son, Ravi.

A lot of people were in love with John at some point and for some reason. Such infatuations can be fleeting, but John's pointed, and often poignant, writing provides a compelling case that our love was not in vain. Though he would write about music, art, science, culture, baseball, and many other things during his too-short life and career, John always returned from whence he came, bearing witness to the aspirations and anxieties of his own lost generation. Like Eve Babitz before him, the Venn Diagram of John's interests and associations is where his best writing and much of the fodder for this collection can be found. Similarly, I hope this book can also provide some reference points and context for those who continue to come here in pursuit of their SoCal dreams, however haunted the endless summer idyll may be.

Haunted. Yes. Despite how funny and matter-of-fact John's writing could be, even in the most extreme circumstances, haunted is an accurate way to describe it. In "The Hep C Generation," for example, published in *Slake: Los Angeles*, John writes about a specter from the past casting a shadow over him and his tribe:

> *I have the virus. So do nearly all my old friends. My best friend from childhood, who I grew up skateboarding and smoking pot with, is infected. The pink-haired pixie from the San Fernando Valley whom I took to my senior prom has it, as does the formerly homeless, nihilist friend with the cigarette burns on his arms who, as an adult, became a wealthy production designer on blockbuster films. In fact, the majority of the kids I knew in the thriving Los Angeles underground of the late seventies and early eighties—from the slam-dancing kids at the Starwood to the young junkies emulating Johnny Thunders outside the Cathay de Grande—have hep c.*
>
> *Now, decades later, as so many of us are finally figuring out how to enjoy our lives, this unwanted remnant from the past keeps surfacing all over town like that half-forgotten friend just released from prison who now insists on hanging out and destroying everything.*

A week or so before he died, John and I had one of those talks wherein we look into the future and can't see too clearly. I told him then that one thing I could say with certainty is that he was one of the very best writers I knew. And I meant it. No matter how tough the subject matter, no matter how rarefied or derelict the company, there was a sweetness in his voice that never left you hanging or put you off. I loved reading him. John demurred and questioned whether it mattered, even if what I said about his writing were true.

I understood. His 2005 memoir *Wrecking Crew: The Really Bad*

News Griffith Park Pirates, a zeitgeist masterpiece in which a crew of ex-punk rockers, recovering drug addicts and cross-dressing brawlers attempt to atone for misspent youths by playing in a fast-pitch, hardball baseball league, had been criminally out of print for years, despite being optioned for the screen several times, including by the late Phillip Seymour Hoffman. In fact, in some dim corner of Hollywood, I'm told, it's still in play. What's more, in this denuded literary landscape, there were fewer and fewer dollars and venues dedicated to the kind of unapologetic interrogation and pinpoint prose at which he excelled. Here's an example from *Wrecking Crew*:

> *My greatest fears in life have always been about isolation and whether I have a place in the world. As a kid, I would sit out on the curb, in my parent's quiet neighborhood at the edge of the desert and listen to the cars as they passed along the nearby highway. The constant sound of motion in the distance only seemed to intensify my feelings of aimlessness and loneliness. The people in those cars had somewhere to go and I did not. Over the years, I've had the same troubling dream in which I take an afternoon nap and sleep until it's dark outside. Still dreaming, I would wake up in a panic and realize that I had no family or friend and nowhere to go, that I was alone. I would try desperately to think of someone to call, and there would be no one. Then, I would actually wake up.*

Nonetheless, during that last phone call, we hypothetically and semi-seriously plotted his return to his hometown of Claremont in order to write the memoir that would pick up what *Wrecking Crew* and the pieces you find here had started to put down: the voice of a generation. Fate had other ideas, and, like Herzog's penguin, we didn't quite get there. But he traveled far and left a lot behind for us. What I offered to John as encouragement during our conversation, I offer to you now as an invitation: that some things matter in ways that are hard to measure. This collection is such a thing and I'm grateful to Iris Berry and Punk Hostage Press for providing the space for this collection. My hope is that what we have done here is preserve for posterity the voice that John gave to the lost sons and daughters of the golden dreamers. It is, as John wrote in "Running With The Devil, A Lifetime of Van Halen:"

> *"...the soundtrack to a world that doesn't exist anymore. I know because that world is where I come from."*

— Joe Donnelly

Foreword

By Ben Harper

It's a Godless universe.

When other words would fail, John would drop this line with the impeccable timing and pinpoint accuracy of a standup comic, hitting the center of the target with clarity and a deep cleansing power. He meant it, too. Not that life was meaningless, or pointless, or lacking in inspiration. No, John was able to see and appreciate the transcendent moments precisely because he refused to over-romanticize life. That was perhaps the most punk-rock aspect of his character and made his input on all things ranging from sports to physics, central to my own perspective. His capacity for razor-sharp insights on culture and human nature, particularly our own, felt scientific to me, as if we were all elements on his personal periodic table.

Growing up, John and I lived next door to each other, 40 miles east of Los Angeles in the college town of Claremont. His mom Julie rang a massive cowbell which hung from a wrought-iron arm bolted to the wall outside their back door. This bell could be heard in every direction for half a mile, signaling all kids in our neighborhood to get home for supper, pronto. (This bell now hangs in my front yard.)

The call to dinner might be the only rule John followed consistently. He always seemed miles ahead of us all, more inclined and more equipped at an earlier age than most of us to challenge our small-town, suburban mores. Yet, he carried his precociousness with humility and gentleness. It wasn't a weapon in his hands the way it can be in some. When he emerged from his backyard at 13 with a picturesque mohawk and a massive safety pin through his left cheek, it was not with aggression, but with calm absolution. When you are preternaturally cool, you have nothing to prove. You are the proof.

I've seen maps that have Claremont as the last city in LA and others where it is the first city in the Inland Empire. Growing up, we always considered it the latter. Either way, back then, the city of Los Angeles seemed unreachable. We had no celebrity kids at our schools. If we wanted stars in the sidewalk, we had to carve them with sticks into the wet cement of our freshly paved walkways. We had zero access to anything special, which forced us to create it.

In 1976, the summer before seventh grade, John and a few fellow budding malcontents began listening to Rodney Bingenheimer on KROQ, where new sounds were starting to invade the increasingly stale classic-rock, album-oriented FM playlists. That next summer, John's parents took the family to London for a holiday. This meant only one thing to John: punk rock.

To this day I'm not sure what I find more astonishing, that in 1977 a 13-year-old from the Inland Empire could find his way to London's legendary 100 club, or that a 13-year-old's father (Bob Albert) would be willing to chaperone him and his brother, Jesse, there. Either way, John found himself in the delivery room for the birth of punk rock in all its stylistic and political insurgency. Upon his return to the Inland Empire, our community, our culture, and our sleepy college town would never be the same, thank God.

And thank you, John.

Running With The Devil: A Lifetime of Van Halen

From Slake*: Los Angeles*

The first time I hear Van Halen I am fourteen years old, riding in a car through the foothills of the San Gabriel Mountains. My friend Steve Darrow is riding shotgun while his dad steers the dusty old Volvo station wagon. Chris Darrow is in his forties and has long hair and a slightly drooping cowboy mustache. In the sixties and early seventies, as a member of the Nitty Gritty Dirt Band and an obscure but influential group called the Kaleidoscope, he, along with Gram Parsons, Linda Ronstadt, and others, forged what became the classic California sound. His long-haired, Black Sabbath–loving son, Steve, sitting shotgun next to him, would go on to play in an early version of Guns N' Roses. But on this particular night Chris is driving us and another friend named Peter home from a party thrown by a local ceramics artist. While the aging hippies and college professors sipped wine and purchased meticulously decorated casserole plates, my friends and I hiked into a nearby orange grove to smoke pot in the moonlight. And as the car heads home along Baseline Boulevard, passing the silhouettes of orange groves and vineyards, the three of us are still incredibly stoned and no one is talking much.

Someone turns on the radio. It's tuned to KROQ, a small, independent station that has little in common with the corporate behemoth it would become. In 1978, the station broadcasts a strange mix of surreal sketch comedy and new music across the Southland. A show called The Hollywood Night Shift riffs on "barbecue bat burgers" and "downhill screen door races." Meanwhile, the station's present-day last man standing, Rodney Bingenheimer, who morning goons Kevin and Bean use as a prop for their moronic shtick, introduces punk music to kids across Southern California. By this time, my friends and I have already fallen under the sway of the raw, new sounds emerging from a ripped, torn, and safety-pin-adorned England.

As we cruise along Baseline, I have no idea what's on the radio. I stare out the window into a passing darkness with hazy, Mexican-weed-induced tunnel vision. Then, suddenly, this extraordinary sound from the car's stereo snaps me back. Steve reaches over and turns up the volume. It's guitar playing, but not like anything we have heard before. Until this very moment, the reigning guitar heroes have been English, amateur warlocks, such as Jimmy Page and Ritchie Blackmore, playing sped-up, bastardized versions of American blues. But this is faster and weirder. Toward the one-minute mark, the playing veers into completely uncharted territory, and the final forty-two seconds sound like Gypsy jazz legend Django Reinhardt after ingesting CIA acid.

It is a style of playing that will so dramatically alter the musical landscape that thirty years later it will sound normal, even rote. But in 1978, this burst of unabashed virtuosity and noise, something we'll later learn is appropriately called "Eruption," earns unexpected respect from three punk rock children and one middle-aged country rock musician. As the whole thing reaches a frenzied crescendo of undulating distortion, the four of us start to laugh.

Until, that is, the distortion immediately segues to a revamped version of the Kinks' classic "You Really Got Me," rumbling through the car's little speakers. This is not hard rock as we know it —no high-pitched, operatic wailing about sorcery or Viking lore. With no visual reference to go on, it seems to have as much in common with early punk as with bands such as Led Zeppelin and Rush—except, of course, for the crazy, outer-space guitar solo. In retrospect, this makes perfect sense. Before it became one of the biggest bands in the world, Van Halen routinely played on bills with prepunk bands like the Runaways, the Mumps, and the Dogs.

When the song ends, Steve's dad, who may or may not be stoned as well, just nods his head and says, "Far out."

***

It is the soundtrack to a world that doesn't exist anymore. I know because that world is where I come from.

Van Halen had been playing the suburbs east of Los Angeles for several years before we heard them on the radio that night. In fact, the previous year, Peter's diminutive, science-teacher mom, who when speaking tended to coo pleasantly like a pigeon, unwittingly supplied Van Halen with several bottles of bourbon and tequila. The occasion was the band's appearance at a show on the local college radio station hosted by Peter's older, but still underage, brother and some of his friends. Following seventies rock etiquette, they felt it only proper to provide the band with alcohol and other recreational substances.

I remember this because my friends and I had been coerced into distributing fliers announcing the band's appearance on the show. Most of our peers glanced at the crudely rendered image of a young David Lee Roth flaunting his soon-to-be legendary chest pelt and bulging package and simply tossed the fliers away. A lot of those same kids would, several years later, pay large sums of money to see the band headline the massive Forum in Inglewood.

In the years leading up to their record deal and worldwide fame, the Internet was still science fiction and the only video game widely available, Pong, mimicked ping-pong only without the riveting excitement and health benefits. As a result, kids were primarily focused on two things, rock music and getting wasted. Days were spent under the sun and smog, getting high, playing sports, skateboarding in empty swimming pools and on downhill streets. Weekend nights were devoted almost entirely to massive backyard parties. And Van

Halen ruled the backyard party scene in and around the San Gabriel Valley.

Unsuspecting parents would leave town and hundreds of kids would descend on a designated home like tanned, stoned locusts. Down the block from my parents' house was a large, ramshackle manor known as the Resort. Sunburned British drunks lived there, and their kids were a wild and eccentric brood bearing names such as Yo-Yo, Kiddy, Sissy, Lad, and Mims.

Parties at the Resort were notorious. I remember watching a formally attired adult couple slow their car in front of the Resort as a party raged inside. Some longhaired kids staggered into the street, walked onto the hood of the couple's car and then its roof, howling like wolves. My preteen friends and I finally mustered the courage to venture inside one of the parties. There, we discovered a maze of hedonistic delights: the dining room table lined with cocaine, a cracked door revealing a nubile high school girl having sex, people jumping from second-story windows into the pool, fights and noisy drag races in the street out front. Throughout the beautifully raucous affair, a young rock 'n' roll band named China White stood precariously close to the swimming pool playing with all the swagger of the Rolling Stones at Madison Square Garden.

While Van Halen played the huge outdoor parties and lucrative high school dances, China White was the band of choice in my immediate neighborhood. The group was composed of young heroin addicts who wore cowboy hats and played Southern rock. Somehow, it was a style that made perfect sense in the slowed-down, drugged-out seventies suburbs. Besides a few performances at the Resort, the band's highest-profile gigs were at the palatial hillside estate of a local ice cream fortune heir. The band's leader, John Dooley, now lives in Bangkok, where he teaches music and plays in a rhythm and blues revue.

"Those were some epic fucking parties," Dooley says when I reach him by phone in Bangkok. "We had a big stage on the tennis courts and the pool house was our backstage area. We invited 500 fellow students, charged a cover, and then got all my older brother's biker buddies to bounce and run screen for the cops. There would be close to a thousand kids there and we would be getting high and fucking chicks in the pool house between sets. I remember we left with our guitar cases stuffed with cash."

But it was with his next band, Mac Pinch, that Dooley's path began to cross regularly with Van Halen's as the two bands shared bills both locally and in Hollywood. "I was always really impressed by Eddie Van Halen and their bass player [Michael Anthony]. They definitely stood out musically, especially Eddie," Dooley says. "Their singer, Roth, was like the guy we had—by no means a great singer, but really loud and worked the crowd well. They used to have a party van with the Van Halen logo painted on the sides, and Roth was always out there in that van. He was kind of obnoxious, but he had a real knack with the ladies. He would bring them out to that van one after another. I had more than my share, but Roth did better than his band and ours combined. We used to play this biker bar in Downey with them called the Downey Outhouse, where they served popcorn in bedpans and beer in urinals.

"It got pretty competitive between the bands, and one time our roadie unplugged Van Halen during a show at the Pasadena Civic."

During these years, roughly 1974 to 1976, Van Halen surpassed all rivals, including San Fernando Valley stars Quiet Riot, to emerge as the premier hard-rock act in Los Angeles. Besides a willingness to play nearly anywhere at any time—the band once played an early-morning breakfast concert at my high school a few years before I attended—the band's rise seemed due, largely, to two distinct qualities. One was the playing of Eddie Van Halen, who had perfected the innovative method of using the fingers of his picking hand to pound the guitar's fretboard, creating a lightning-fast, quasi-classical style that quickly became the talk of Southland musicians. Van Halen reportedly became so guarded about this technique that he began to play solos with his back to the audience.

And while the teenage boys came to marvel at Eddie's technical virtuosity, the girls flocked to see the band's flamboyant lead singer. David Lee Roth would take the stage shirtless, wearing skin-tight spandex pants or fur-lined assless chaps, none of which dampened his enthusiasm for jumping into the air and doing karate kicks and splits. Visually, Roth resembled a stoner superhero with his wild, long blond hair, muscular physique, and exaggerated party bravado. But what set him apart from so many aspiring frontmen of the time, was that, unbeknownst to his mostly blond-haired, blue-eyed audience, Roth was Jewish. And though his father was a wealthy ophthalmologist, young Roth went to public schools and ended up attending primarily black John Muir High in Pasadena. As a result, he was able to merge an over-the-top, borscht-belt-like showmanship with the booty-shaking sex appeal of his Funkadelicized classmates. It was a combination that made Roth a near-perfect rock star for those hedonistic times.

While Van Halen's star rose, my friends Dooley and Mac Pinch were on a different trajectory. Instead of showcasing alongside their one-time rivals at Hollywood clubs such as the Starwood and the Whisky, the drug-addled young cowboys started booking USO tours and playing military bases to support their various nonmusical habits. When Van Halen finally had its big breakthrough and signed to Warner Bros. Records, Mac Pinch was off playing to halls of drunken Marines.

"Those were serious smack days for me," Dooley reflects. "Eventually it all caught up to me and I had to come back home and do some jail time, and that was the end of the band." I ask him if he has regrets after seeing his former rivals go on to such massive success.

"Do I think we should have tried harder? That maybe it could have been us?" he offers. "Sure. But we had a lot of fun playing those parties. I have some great memories. It was a pretty awesome time to be young and playing in a rock 'n' roll band."

***

Two years after first hearing Van Halen on the car radio, the world around me seems a dramatically different place. My once long hair is now short and jagged and I'm wearing studded wristbands with a spider-shaped earring punched through an infected hole in my ear. In suburbs across Southern California, punk rockers have swelled from a besieged minority to an increasingly aggressive subculture. There are pervasive hostilities between the heavy-metal-loving "stoners" and the new punks. Both sides instigate violence. By now, I have been expelled from the local high school for truancy and am enrolled in something called Claremont Collegiate Academy. Despite its snooty name, the place is filled with kids who have failed at the local high schools. My classmates are mainly longhaired drug users, agitated Iranian immigrants, and kids with assorted behavioral disorders. The principal will eventually be arrested on child porn charges.

During one lunch break, I stroll out into the school parking lot and am greeted by the pounding, tribal drums of Van Halen's latest single, "Everybody Wants Some," blasting from the open doors of a huge four-wheel-drive truck. Two very attractive teenage girls stand on the truck's roof, dancing to the music. Both are outfitted in tight, shimmering spandex pants, halter tops, and moon boots. They bump their perfectly shaped asses together and sing along with David Lee Roth: "Everybody wants some/I want some too/Everybody wants some, baby, how 'bout you." As I walk by, a girl with feathered blond hair points at me and sneers, seductively, singing, "Everybody wants some, baby, how 'bout you?"

I do.

A week later, I end up ditching school with the monster truck's down-jacket-wearing owner and the two dancing girls. We drive into the nearby mountains to sip Southern Comfort and smoke pot. The girls tell me that Van Halen singer David Lee Roth is a "super fox" and they both desperately want to fuck him. On the drive home, I'm in the truck's back seat making out with the blond girl. Her lip gloss tastes like raspberry candy. I caress her nipples through her shirt and eventually slip a finger between her legs, which seems like a monumental achievement. I stop when I realize she has fallen asleep in my arms. A few days later, she pulls me into an unoccupied darkroom between classes and we fondle one another for a few seconds. After several more brief flirtations, the pull of our opposing camps is just too much and we eventually stop talking. A year later, I run into her at a local hamburger stand, where she works behind the counter. She hands me my food and waves me off before I can pay.

***

I'm an eighteen-year-old in the basement of a Hollywood nightclub called the Cathay De Grande. Slumped in an empty booth, my eyes are closed and my head rests on the table. Fifteen minutes earlier, I injected heroin inside the cramped restroom with the sound man. It is a Monday night and a local blues outfit called Top Jimmy and the Rhythm Pigs are on the small stage. They are fronted by a white-trash blues legend, Top Jimmy, and play the club every Monday night. The place is nearly empty. The Rhythm Pigs are cool, but like most in attendance, I am really here to score drugs. This accomplished, I nod off, lost in some distant dream world as the band plays their hearts out just a few feet away.

When I eventually drift back to reality, something odd catches my ear. Instead of Top Jimmy's throaty voice, someone lets loose with an exaggerated, arena-rock scream. Perplexed, I lift my head and focus on the small stage. There, sandwiched between the band's rotund bass player and slovenly guitar player, Carlos Guitarlos, is none other than David Lee Roth, holding the microphone and striking a majestic rock pose. It's surreal seeing one of the most successful singers in the world standing in this dilapidated basement club alongside a bunch of musicians teetering on the brink of homelessness and liver failure.

"Whoa-bop-ditty-doobie-do-bop, oh yeah, baby!" Roth yells out, putting his arm around an inebriated Top Jimmy. As bleary-eyed Jimmy leans in and begins to sing, Roth watches him with a beaming smile, clapping his hands and laughing in exaggerated-but-sincere appreciation. "Top-motherfucking Jimmy!" he yells out, as if addressing a sold-out arena instead of several stunned junkies and alcoholics. The reaction from the sparse crowd is indifference bordering on hostility. There is nothing less cool in the Hollywood underground than a seemingly happy millionaire rock star. But Top Jimmy is smiling with his arm around Roth. And a few years later, when Van Halen releases its multiplatinum-selling record *1984*, the album features a track called "Top Jimmy."

"Top Jimmy cooks, Top Jimmy swings, Top Jimmy—he's the king," Roth sings in tribute to his friend, who would eventually die of liver failure.

***

The next two decades are a creative dark age for Van Halen. After years of ego-fueled turmoil from all sides, David Lee Roth leaves the band to pursue a doomed solo career. An entirely unremarkable singer named Sammy Hagar replaces him and Van Halen becomes one of the most boring bands in existence. Roth recedes from the limelight, studying martial arts and making an ill-fated stab as a radio deejay.

Eddie's excessive drinking begins to take a toll. One night in 1993 at the height of the grunge years, a drunken Eddie appears backstage for a Nirvana concert at the Forum. He reportedly begs Kurt Cobain to let him join the band on stage, explaining, "I'm all washed up; you are what's happening now." He also, for unexplained reasons, supposedly sniffs Cobain's deodorant before calling Nirvana's half-black rhythm guitarist Pat Smear a "Mexican" and a "Raji." Needless to say, he is not allowed on stage.

In the following years, news of Van Halen is sporadic, largely unsubstantiated, and generally not positive. One story has Eddie sitting in with guitarless rap-rock buttheads Limp Bizkit. When they are slow to return his prized equipment, Eddie supposedly goes back with automatic weapons. An acquaintance of mine who sells rare guitars does some business with Eddie and subsequently receives lonely, rambling, late night phone calls from him. An old friend who is now a teacher hosts a day for his students to bring in their grandparents. One student inexplicably brings in Eddie Van Halen. He stays for hours, politely talking to the kids about his Dutch heritage and childhood music studies.

During this time, Roth is arrested in a New York City park for purchasing weed. And when a meth-addled man attempts a wee-hours break-in at the singer's Pasadena mansion, the intruder is surprised to find "Diamond Dave" wide awake and at the ready. Some accounts have Roth training a gun on the intruder while others have the lifelong martial-arts enthusiast, resplendent in silk pajamas, subduing the man with a lightening-fast nunchuck demonstration.

But as the years pass, "important" bands like Nirvana feel increasingly dated while the celebratory party anthems of Roth-era Van Halen continue to dominate the airwaves. Their songs are played repeatedly every day on multiple stations throughout the civilized world. And after several well-publicized misfires including an aborted reunion and a stint with a much-maligned singer named Gary

Cherone, Eddie Van Halen and David Lee Roth finally find their way back to each other in 2007. The group announces it will be hitting the road, though original bassist Michael Anthony is to be replaced by Eddie's sixteen-year-old son, Wolfgang, who reportedly suggested the tour and persuaded his dad to reconcile with Roth. What ensues is the band's highest grossing tour to date.

I catch Van Halen's show at the gleaming new Staples Center in downtown L.A., anticipating a heartfelt homecoming. Instead, I get a slick and entertaining professional rock show. There are no missteps, but little if anything seems spontaneous. Then, leading into the song "Ice Cream Man," Roth stops and delivers a monologue. I later learn from watching videos online that it's pretty much the same speech in every city. Still, it has particular significance in Los Angeles, mere miles from where it all started. "The suburbs, I come from the suburbs," Roth says to the cheering crowd. "You know, where they tear out the trees and name streets after them. I live on Orange Grove—there's no orange grove there; it's just me. In fact, most of us in the band come from the suburbs and we used to play the backyard parties there. … I remember it like it was yesterday."

***

Not long ago, I'm at my parents' house in those very suburbs, visiting with my dad, who is slowly dying, his body wasting away. After leaving his house, I stop for gas. As I stand at the pump, a tall, disheveled man approaches me. He begins to ask for spare change, then stops and stares at me. After a moment, he says my name. I look back blankly and he awkwardly introduces himself. It turns out that we grew up together. The once-handsome and talented athlete has been drinking hard and using cocaine, and his life has unraveled in dramatic fashion. The last I'd heard, he was living behind a local bar in an abandoned camper shell but was asked to leave for having too many guests and making too much noise. I ask how he is and he just shakes his head. I take out my wallet and offer a twenty, which he refuses. I insist, and he eventually palms the bill and slides it into a pocket. After some strained small talk, he asks for a ride to a friend's apartment. I reluctantly agree.

The two of us drive through the streets of our shared childhood in awkward silence. The orange groves have long since turned into a sprawl of tract housing and circuitous dead ends, both literal and figurative. I turn on the radio, scan stations, and eventually stop on Van Halen's 1978 classic "Ain't Talkin' 'Bout Love." I turn up the volume. After a few seconds, the propulsive guitar riff fades down and David Lee Roth begins to talk.

"I been to the edge, an' there I stood an' looked down/You know I lost a lot of friends there, baby, I got no time to mess around."

The music builds in intensity before exploding into a powerful, defiant chorus: "Ain't talkin' 'bout love, my love is rotten to the core/Ain't talkin' 'bout love, just like I told you before, before, before/Hey hey hey!" By this time, my old friend is singing along and pumping his fist in the air. His eyes are moist from either alcohol, sadness, or both. The song finishes just as we pull in front of a dilapidated apartment complex, and he climbs out. He hesitates and looks in at me.

"Hey man, remember those crazy parties back in the day?" I nod and force a smile. "Those were some good fucking times," he says, reaching in and slapping my shoulder affectionately before disappearing into the darkness.

The Satori Underground: King Crimson

From the anthology *Yes Is The Answer And Other Prog-Rock Tales.*

If the renowned progressive rock band King Crimson conveyed a sense of epic grandeur and complexity, on that morning, my friend Dwight and I were at the opposite end of the universe. Two 16-year-old heroin addicts standing in a fenced-in patch of dried cracked dirt and tumbleweeds in the backyard of his mom's home on the edge of the Southern California desert. He was tall and black and I was white and blond. The sun was burning through a haze of thick smog that emanated from the massive nearby Kaiser Steel plant and we were each wearing a thrift store suit.

The neighborhood was a bleak approximation of the suburban dream —a cheaply constructed, recently erected, stucco slum for the working poor fleeing the gang violence and crime of nearby Los Angeles. A section of houses towards the back of the tract had been unofficially designated for black people and so that's where Dwight and his single mother Rosa were living. It was also where I had been staying after running away from my parent's tree-shaded and book-filled home in the nearby college town of Claremont. Like so many restless middle-class teenagers, I had rejected a world of comfort and access for an exotic sense of downward mobility.

Dwight and I had met a year before our freshman year of high school. He had moved in with his grandmother in an apartment near my parents' house. Most of our classmates had long feathered hair and wore casual surfwear even though we were miles from the beach. Dwight joined a small group of us who bonded over a shared love for aggressive punk music, alcohol, and vandalism. From there things had progressed accordingly. A year later, we had both been expelled from school, begun injecting Mexican heroin and listening to the artier and dissonant sounds of post-punk—a genre that included bands like Throbbing Gristle, Public Image Ltd, Blurt and Killing Joke.

Squinting and sweating in the desert heat that day, we stared off across a barren field of scrub towards a small bar attached to a bowling alley. There were several choppers parked outside, one draped with a leather jacket adorned with a patch reading "Devils Disciples MC, Southern Cal."

"You can get it," Dee told me. "You're fast. I have complete confidence."

"Those Vikings would lasso me with a chain before I got halfway back," I replied.

"That jacket's worth at least five hundred on Melrose. We'll be high for days."

"Then you fucking do it."

"Always trying to get the black man to do your dirty work," he said with a laugh, taking a hit off a joint and passing it to me. He reached down and pressed play on a large, battered ghetto blaster. The futuristic sound of the David Bowie song "Heroes" filled the little yard. "Heroes" is the title song from Bowie's 1977 album of the same name. Recorded in Berlin it features a stark and atmospheric sound created by Bowie and co-writer Brian Eno. The sonic centerpiece of the song is a futuristic dissonant guitar played by Robert Fripp, a founding member of the aforementioned King Crimson.

Neither Dwight nor I were fans of King Crimson or any other even remotely progressive rock bands. When punk came along, me and my pot-smoking skateboarding friends, like a cadre of prepubescent rock Maoists, had obliterated the past in order to rewrite our musical landscape. Taking a cue from Sex Pistol singer Johnny Rotten who had once marched through London in a homemade "(I hate) Pink Floyd" shirt, once-cherished bands like Led Zeppelin had abruptly been deemed irrelevant dinosaurs while mainstream prog rock practitioners like Yes and Rush with their virtuoso musicianship and escapist fantasy themes had become objects of outright derision.

Yet we continued to revere David Bowie. While his signature glitter albums predated and influenced punk, his subsequent Berlin-era records; *Low*, *Heroes* and *Lodger* helped usher in the post-punk movement that perfectly mirrored our personal descents into teenage nihilism and deadly addiction. This was relevant because Fripp and Adrian Belew, another guitarist who played on Bowie's album *Lodger* and with Bowie's band during the *Stage* tour of 1978, were scheduled to perform that November night in 1981 with a reformed version of King Crimson. Dwight and I planned to go.

***

The closest I had come to seeing a prog rock show before that had been years before when I was 12 and a bunch of my friends had stolen some wine and gone to a local revival screening of the Yes concert film *Yessongs*. After consuming much of the bottle concealed in my jacket, I had loudly addressed the theater full of bearded hippies, accusing the band's cape-adorned keyboardist Rick Wakeman of being a warlock. Why I thought that was news to anyone can only be attributed to the naiveté of youth and the pilfered Zinfandel. After another outburst regarding Yes singer Jon Anderson being a eunuch, the theater's ushers appeared and threw us out as the surrounding long hairs applauded.

But by the age of sixteen, we were doing everything possible to distance ourselves from such innocent hijinks. For some inexplicable reason, my friends and I wanted desperately to be old and jaded. For me, the oppressive stillness of the Southern California suburbs and an inner emotional turmoil resulted in a painful restlessness. For others, including Dwight, there were also broken homes. All this merged with above-average intellects to create a hunger for adventure which drew us to new music and literature, but also a destructive underworld of drugs and crime. And so instead of skateboarding and kissing girls, we spent our teenage years using heroin and dressing like middle-aged criminals from some dreary nonexistent European city of another era.

That night as we drove the freeway in Dwight's mom's old Chevy Camaro, he slipped in a cassette of Brian Eno's solo album *Here Come The Warm Jets*. The mix of theatrical glitter rock and dissonant futurism merged perfectly with the scenery outside as the barren desert turned to sprawling suburbia and then the lights and violent chaos of Los Angeles.

We exited the freeway onto Hollywood Boulevard and headed towards Western. Back then the intersection of Hollywood and Western was a bustling outdoor bazaar of drugs and prostitution. We slowed to survey the scene outside. The song playing was "Baby's on Fire," a tension-filled track where Eno sings in a mocking sneer accompanied by a beautifully violent guitar solo from Robert Fripp.

"That's my dad," Dwight suddenly said, pointing out the window to a crowd in front of an adult bookstore. I spotted a tall, forty-something African American man standing on the corner wearing a white captain's hat with the calm confident demeanor of a dangerous man.

"Are you serious?" I asked.

"Yeah."

Years later I would find out that Dwight's mom had lived in constant fear that her son would someday reconnect with his career-criminal father, anticipating the pull his presence might have on her gifted but troubled son.

We parked and walked to where his dad was standing. The two greeted one another with smiles. Dwight introduced us.

"So, what you young men doing out here in Hollywood?" His father asked.

"Going up to Pasadena and see a band—was looking to go downtown first," Dwight answered, using an old-time slang term for heroin.

"I see.... Well, there ain't none around here," his dad responded. "Maybe over on the Eastside—I'll take a ride with you if you want, but I can't guarantee we'll find anything."

"You got anything else?" Dwight asked.

"Got some loads—doors and fours," he answered, referring to a powerful and potentially lethal combination of Codeine and Doriden that had become popular in the black community and was gaining traction in the Hollywood punk scene. Doriden was a powerful tranquilizer that enabled the body to convert the codeine to morphine.

"They're pills, right?" Dwight asked, noticeably disappointed.

"Put your head in your chest better than the strongest her-ron will," his father said, putting a hand on Dwight's shoulder and smiling. "I wouldn't steer you wrong, son. Give 'em to you for what they cost me, cause we're family."

***

A half-hour later, Dwight and I were in a grassy park across the street from the theater. The marquee read "King Crimson" with the band members' names—Adrian Belew, Bill Bruford, Robert Fripp, Tony Levin—spelled out below. We washed down the pills with a bottle of King Cobra malt liquor and watched the crowd. The people filing into the venue were vastly different than the jaded, black-clad Hollywood scenesters we were used to. They appeared a mix of serious musician types and aging hippies. Having neither tickets nor money, we walked around to the backstage door of the theater and asked for a guy we knew. Dennis was a part-time bouncer from my parent's neighborhood—a hulking long haired giant with a bushy beard and a metal plate in his head from a botched suicide attempt with a pellet gun. That night he smiled the two of us in, teasing that we were finally going to hear what he deemed some "real" music. A year later Dennis would publicly vow to kill me, believing incorrectly that I had burglarized the house, but would overdose and die before he could make good on his threat.

Once inside Dwight and I pushed through the crowd and stood in the orchestra pit just beneath the stage. After a bit the houselights dimmed, the crowd cheered and four musicians strolled out looking like new-wave college professors. They took their places and began to play a song called "Frippertronics." Accustomed to the theatrical bombast of hard rock and the unrestrained aggression of punk, the complex math rock being played was completely foreign to us. While the rest of the audience seemed to marvel at the musicianship on display, Dwight and I were lost. It felt more like a loud academic presentation than the Bowie adjacent performance we were expecting.

Like the pills we had recently ingested, the effects of King Crimson took a while for us to feel. As the synthetic warmth of the narcotics began to spread through our teenage bloodstreams, the group launched into a song called "Sartori In Tangier," the title referencing Tangier, a favorite destination in the fifties for beat writers such as Paul Bowles, William S. Burroughs and Allen Ginsburg.

The song started out slow and atmospheric, then the bass came in like a syncopated ultra-heavy frantic version of funk. The band was suddenly playing with a newfound urgency, pounding drums and bass propelling the music with a jagged tension. Dwight, who had grown up listening to his mother's R&B and had embraced Parliament and Rick James and then the "no wave" funk of James Chance and Blurt, got it before I did. I looked over and saw him doing a herky-jerky new wave-like dance resembling one of the violently twisting suit and tie characters from artist Robert Longo's "Men in the Cities" series.

I remember laughing in appreciation of my friend's absolute fuck-everything abandon. Then I began to move as well. As a cynical white suburban intellectual, I had never been much of a dancer. But the pills provided an overwhelming sense of well-being that allowed me to lose myself in the moment and the sound. And so there I was gyrating next to my friend. No one else in the audience was dancing. Amidst a sea of long-haired nodding heads, were two young suit-adorned punks flailing around. I have a blurry, perhaps hallucinatory, vision of Adrian Belew smiling down at us from the stage. Whether that is true or not, I still believe the point of the band in that incarnation was the power of its beautiful and exotic noise.

After a few minutes, Robert Fripp let loose with a solo unlike any guitar I had ever heard. It was a frenetic and beautifully evocative wall of noise that conveyed both an otherworldly exoticism and a profound sense of yearning. At some point I smiled and closed my eyes, the sound stirring visions of Tangier-like landscapes in my brain.

***

When I eventually woke up, Dwight was driving the car back into the desert as the sun rose. I remember thinking that he looked old in his suit, staring out at the road with heavy-lidded eyes. I faded out again and when I regained consciousness it was the afternoon and I was in Dwight's mom's house. I wandered into the backyard. Dwight was sitting in a lawn chair holding a guitar. His six-year-old brother Selino was next to him listening as his big brother played the David Bowie song "Heroes," singing the words in a raspy whisper: "We can beat them—forever and ever, we can be heroes—just for one day."

Dwight died just a few years later. As his mother had feared, he returned to Hollywood and reconnected with his father. The two had lived with a roving band of thieves, dealers, and prostitutes in the motels around Hollywood while his dad schooled him in the criminal life. The afternoon of his death, Dwight was sharing a jail cell with his dad. Both of them were facing separate life sentences for different drug-related murders. At twenty-one years old, Dwight took a rope he had constructed out of bed sheets and climbed out an eleventh-story window. He lost his grip and slipped away.

Decades after that, I was riding through Los Angeles in the back of a sleek Mercedes with a famous and rich rock star I was interviewing. As we drove into the Hollywood Hills, he put on the King Crimson album "In the Court of the Crimson King." The epic music played loudly and I began to think about the band and then my friend. In the silence between songs, the rock star had looked at the lights below and asked if I had grown up in Los Angeles. I told him I had.

Black Flag, Hong Kong Café

From *The Show I'll Never Forget: 50 Writers Relive Their Most Memorable Concertgoing Experiences.*

The Los Angeles suburbs. It is a landscape of glaring sunlight filtered through brown, hazy smog. The streets are nearly always empty—a meandering maze of unending sameness lined with manicured lawns and identical box-like houses. The majority of kids at my school are tanned with feathered hair. They wear casual beach-wear, though we are thirty miles from the ocean. The good kids listen to the somnambulistic sounds of Jackson Brown and The Eagles and campaign against nuclear power. The bad kids listen to Van Halen and what's left of Led Zeppelin and worship all things weed. I despise it all (except the drugs). I have cut my hair short and can't stop smashing windows.

I am not alone. A small, disgruntled cadre of us have embraced punk rock. We no longer even go to school, instead spending our days at the unsupervised homes of friends, getting wasted and listening to records. I have been in trouble since grade school—mainly vandalism, shoplifting, and drugs. Recently the school board has sent a letter home informing my parents that I am to be expelled for chronic truancy. My father has stopped talking to me, and my mom wears the same shell-shocked expression as Ellen Burstyn playing the mother in *The Exorcist*. They consult a psychiatrist; I am given medication. I crush up a month's supply of the pills and snort them with my friends. That night I stay awake grinding my teeth, listening to the dissonant new album by Public Image Ltd. and jerking off. As a diplomatic concession, I agree to attend a group for troubled adolescents in nearby Orange County. I befriend the other patients and we are soon getting stoned in a nearby vacant lot before therapy sessions. I manage to finger a blond-haired surfer girl in the restroom. Months later I see her at an Orange County punk festival. Her hair is blue, and she is wearing a swastika armband.

I love punk rock, but know it is a fantasy. We are not in England. My family is not poor. It is not raining. I can relate to the rebellion and anger of the music, and sometimes try to imagine I am in London, but it's difficult. The sun is too bright and there is silence all around. Each night I sit on the curb outside my parents' house and listen to the sound of cars passing in the distance. There is a growing panic inside me. I can't shake the thought that somewhere else there is something exciting and profound happening—and I am missing it all.

There is definitely something happening in nearby Hollywood. We hear about it every Sunday night on the radio. For two hours each week, an elfin little man named Rodney Bingenheimer plays the latest punk records and raves about all the cool shows happening in town. My friends and I occasionally make it into the city, usually to see bigger English bands like The Clash and The Damned. But none of us drive yet and our parents are no longer an option since we are all technically grounded forever. The only way is to find someone older and convince them to take us—which is difficult since we despise nearly everyone. There is a well-meaning student from the nearby Claremont College who has driven us a few times. She has a punk radio show on the college station, but when she invites us to be on her show, we lock her out of the room, spray paint the walls, steal records, and yell obscenities over the airwaves. She remains bitter.

My friend Roger and I are trying desperately to start a band, which we plan on calling Christian Death. So far it is just the two of us huddled in my parents' musty garage plucking away on a cheap bass and guitar. Roger goes by the name Xerox Clone, though he will later call himself Rozz Williams and amass a worldwide following before hanging himself. But at this time, he is just a pimply-faced punk rocker in engineer boots and studded wristbands. He tells me there's a punk show he wants to see the following Sunday at a club called the Hong Kong Café in Chinatown. My initial thought is that going out on a Sunday just means a further escalation in the war with my parents. Then I think that things can't possibly get any worse—so why not? We need a ride. The next day a few of us are sitting around when someone suggests we call Carol. Everyone sort of fidgets and then exhales in fatalistic resignation.

Carol works at a local record store and fancies herself punk. She is significantly older, in her early twenties, and is considered by us to be new-wave and a total skank. Several months later when The Ramones play the Garrison Theater on the campus of the Claremont Colleges, Carol confiscates her store's promotional tickets and sits front row in a short skirt. When the band takes the stage, Carol promptly lifts her legs in the air and flashes her beaver. Even from my position towards the back, I can make out expressions of horror on Joey and Dee Dee's faces. Nevertheless, Carol is our only candidate. So, Roger, who even as a teenager possesses a subtle and powerful charisma, calls her and she agrees.

Sunday night, I exit my room wearing a tattered black suit and thick eyeliner and announce that I am simply "going out." As I start for the door, my mom suddenly blocks my path and tells me, "No." My dad walks out of the bathroom and pins me with a steely stare, jaw clenching and face reddening.

"You're not going anywhere, goddammit," he says, seething with controlled rage, disappointment, and concern.

The three of us heatedly debate the topic. As if following some internal prime directive, my adolescent fury starts to build. Decades later, after extensive therapy both court-motivated and elective, I can now explain the intricate forces that compelled me towards such destructive behavior. But for purposes of this story, none of that really matters. What *is* important is that it was not a choice. It wasn't done for effect or as a rebellious pose. If I could have been happy and well-adjusted, I would have done so in a heartbeat. But standing there in my parents' kitchen with everyone shouting, I lose control, flail around, and kick out a small window. Then I am out the door and gone.

As I walk through the darkness to meet up with my friends, I don't feel good. Deep down I can sense my life heading somewhere unpleasant and dark. I feel lost and actually a bit scared. But I also know if I can get some alcohol in me things will feel significantly better, at least until the morning.

I wait at the designated street corner studying every approaching headlight. Being a punk in those years was a perilous endeavor. Besides traumatized parents and overly suspicious police, there was the constant possibility that grown men in pickup trucks will arbitrarily pull over and attack. Earlier that year a group of middle-aged tree trimmers attacked my friends in a local park. In a stunning upset, my young pals beat the rednecks until the men tearfully apologized and ran away. But on this night, I feel vulnerable and sincerely glad to hear my friends' catcalls as they pull up in Carol's dented-up little Toyota.

Carol is dressed as a punk schoolgirl. Roger rides shotgun with his hair freshly dyed black. In the backseat is my childhood friend Peter, an x carved into his forehead, and Dee—who is even further marginalized as a black punk rocker. Dee is undeniably tough, though. A few years later he will reunite with his pimp father, rob some banks and die trying to escape from jail. But on this night, packed into the little car speeding towards the city, the world seems filled with promise. The vodka and orange juice Carol has purchased doesn't hurt, either.

A half-hour later we are pulling off the freeway and cutting through the neon-lit streets of Chinatown. We park, pile out into a narrow alleyway smelling of Chinese food and bum urine, and finish what remains of the vodka. The nearby Hong Kong Cafe is actually a converted Chinese banquet hall upstairs from a little bar. By the time we bound up the stairs, the four of us are brimming with drunken, youthful bravado. Carol, meanwhile, ducks into the downstairs bar for a few more drinks.

***

The punk rock scene in Los Angeles consists mainly of drugged-out art school types and ex-glam rock fans who have cut their hair upon hearing the Sex Pistols. Actual kids like us are still somewhat of a rarity, though the five members of Red Cross—the first band up—are even younger than we are. I have heard them on Rodney's radio show. Their guitar player is an awkward-looking kid named Greg Hetson who will go on to form the Circle Jerks. The two of us will also play together in the band Bad Religion for a stint. I remember him on this night because some drunk bounces an empty beer can off his head as he plays and he never even glances up. As Red Cross finish, Carol reemerges from the downstairs bar looking significantly more inebriated and trailed by an equally drunk and quite smitten Chinese man.

None of us have heard of the next band, and as they set up their equipment, they certainly don't look very punk. No spiky hair, bondage pants, or leather jackets, they seem more like guys who would live in their parents' garage and smoke a lot of weed. Eventually, their singer strolls on to the stage. He is a small, nondescript guy wearing an oversized army jacket and holding a can of Budweiser. When he leans forward and speaks into the mic, it is with a distinctively SoCal drawl—just like every fucked-up kid I have ever known.

"Heeey man, we're Black Flag..."

They start playing, and it's as if someone has jammed a syringe into my neck and injected the purest Crystal Methedrine. One minute we're milling about checking out the Hollywood girls, next there's this blistering wall of sound blasting from the small stage. Everyone is just stunned. It is punk rock, but not like before. This is faster and angrier. Over the next few years, Black Flag will alter the American musical landscape. But what's important this particular night is that it's music made specifically for us. Keith Morris isn't up there singing about political injustice or class oppression; he's screaming about the exact kind of pain and frustration we are feeling.

I'm about to have a nervous breakdown.

My head really hurts.

And within seconds everyone is careening around the dance floor. Slam dancing (initially called "The Huntington Beach Strut" and later "moshing") hasn't been invented yet, but we're not exactly pogo-ing either. We're really just—going off. Everything after that is kind of a blur. Some guys attack a smaller guy and Dee jumps in and starts swinging. I soon have a black eye, but not from that particular melee. In my excitement, I turn and joyously hurl Carol across a nearby table. She promptly circles back and unleashes a solid haymaker into the side of my face.

***

After the show, we stand bruised and elated outside the club in a little tourist square. The riotous music has somehow given our confused lives a fleeting sense of purpose. Carol, on the other hand, is so drunk she can hardly walk. Her Chinese suitor has at last given up and fallen asleep on a bench beside a koi pond. By the time we reach the car, Carol is unconscious. Thankfully, the transmission is automatic. Roger bravely volunteers to drive. We pile in and nervously watch as the fifteen-year-old future "King of Goth" tentatively merges the car onto the eastbound freeway and back towards the suburbs.

A half-hour later I am standing outside my parents' house. All the lights are off. There is a note taped to the back door. It reads simply, "Go away." I try the door. It is locked. I trudge into the front yard and start calling my older brother's name while tossing pebbles at his bedroom window. I am more than a little startled when he sheepishly pokes his head out of the shrub next to me.

"What do you want?"

It turns out he and his friends had taken some unexpectedly potent LSD and gone to see the new movie *Alien*. It was not the laugh-fest they had anticipated, and he has been huddled in the bush for hours.

The next morning my family convenes at the breakfast table. It is an understandably tense affair. My parents don't mention my black eye or the window I had broken the night before. In fact, they don't say a word. We all just eat in silence—except for my brother, who stares at his food and coos softly like a pigeon. I quickly leave for school, but a few blocks away decide not to go. There doesn't really seem any point. Instead, I meet my friends at an abandoned baseball dugout where we drink beer and recount the previous night's adventure. Weeks later I come across Black Flag's first three-song EP at the local record store—and steal it.

Man Goes Home To Mom

From the LA Weekly

Several weeks ago, my neighbor Larry abruptly told me he was moving away. He said he didn't want to but could no longer afford the soaring rents in our Silver Lake neighborhood combined with a now–nearly nonexistent job market. The sadness I felt upon hearing this took me a little by surprise. I liked Larry, but it's not like we were the best of friends. Though he only lived 15 feet from me, I had never once set foot in his apartment. Regardless, I had come to count on him. He was a neighborhood institution of sorts, like the colorful restaurant or bar you have never bothered to patronize but are then sad to see close. It seemed for the past decade or so that Larry could be found perched outside Café Tropical, drinking coffee and talking with the other regulars. He was informed on topics ranging from sports to politics and was an invaluable source of neighborhood gossip. I can't remember attending a local function in the past decade that featured a free bar and did not also feature Larry. He would be missed.

In the big picture, Larry's departure seemed further proof that the world around me was changing, and for the worse. I had seen many local institutions disappear over the years. While some left undeniable holes in the community, many of the changes had initially seemed to be for the better. I enjoyed many of the new highbrow restaurants, for instance, and, having been caught in more than one gang-related shootout, welcomed the decrease in crime that came with gentrification. But the neighborhood had also ceased to be the affordable refuge for creative misfits it had been when I initially moved here from Hollywood in the late '80s. After countless profiles heralding Silver Lake as some sort of West Coast mecca of cool, rents in the area soon rivaled those on the Westside. And when the recent financial crisis wiped out many of the once-plentiful film production jobs, the result was a perfect storm for valued ne'er-do-wells like Larry.

When I eventually tracked Larry down, he told me that he had survived over the years by doing an assortment of jobs designed to fund creative endeavors that have ranged from playing in bands to writing for film and television. "Everything that I have done to make money has been to support the creative work," he said. "I've done script-reading, house-painting, set-decorating, management in a food-and-beverage venture, and some things I can't really mention here. I call it all my work compost. When you've lived somewhere long enough, you know what it takes to get by. But all that's trickier now. There's less freelance money around. It's not just large institutions that have to rethink how to survive. It's also average people like me, who had relied on a climate that allowed you to pursue your art and make a living at the same time."

The two of us were talking over burritos in the heart of the San Fernando Valley. If Larry's exodus from the neighborhood hadn't given me pause, his destination certainly had. It wasn't the fact that he was living in the Valley, where he grew up. What troubled me was that, in his 40s, Larry was now back home living with his parents. To be honest, my reaction had far more to do with my own fears. Larry seemed pretty upbeat about the situation, but for me, it conjured a haunting figure from my childhood known as "Pete the Hippie." An intelligent and harmless man in his 30s with a non-ironic beard, Pete lived at home with his elderly parents, doing ceramics and with neighborhood kids (including myself) smoking pot out of a winged bong. I have since lived in near-constant fear of somehow ending up a less-hirsute version of Pete. Larry noted my downbeat demeanor and confronted me.

"Look, this isn't some sad story, John," he stated. "My circumstances are difficult, but I don't want to read something about me being all down on my luck. There is a total upside to my situation. It gives me an opportunity to make adjustments to my life. And I think a lot of people are re-evaluating what they are doing now, from people with high-paying positions to guys like me, who have been able to string together a compost of jobs."

Larry relaxed, leaned back, and smiled. "And look, I'm getting the opportunity to do things I would never have done back in Silver Lake. Like eating popcorn and watching *Dancing With The Stars* with my mom."

I imagined the scene, a bathrobe-clad mother and her 40-something Berkeley graduate son sitting in front of the television watching Lil' Kim do the rumba. It troubled me. "You sit on the couch with your mom and watch *Dancing With The Stars*?" I asked, my voice rising to a controlled shriek.

Larry shook his head with dismay. "Dude, I'm not on the couch with her. She's on the couch. I'm nearby luxuriating on the comfy rug."

We finished our burritos and walked to a local coffeehouse. It felt like a million miles from Larry's old haunt in Silver Lake. Instead of framed Che Guevara posters, there were expensive gift baskets for purchase, and the baristas looked like soap opera actors. It hit me that Larry was in no danger of becoming a modern Pete the Hippie. Besides the fact that he was relatively clean-shaven and seemed totally uninterested in pottery, Larry said he was working harder than ever now. He had several jobs, including tutoring kids for bar mitzvahs (his dad was a cantor), and was saving his money. He also told me the shift had intensified his focus on his own work. Far from pathetic, there was actually something inspiring about how he was handling a situation many of us could easily face. Still, I would miss seeing him around the neighborhood.

"I'm not sitting on my hands," Larry said. "I know this is a hard time to get things done. But I'm also relatively optimistic. I believe in what I'm doing and I have huge expectations. In fact, I've brokered a life based on expectations. But for now—popcorn and *Dancing With The Stars*."

Chaz Bojorquez, Beyond The Streets

From *Beyond The Streets*

Back in 1969, within the monolithic concrete canyons and tunnels of the LA River that runs through Northeast Los Angeles, a symbol began to appear on the walls. It was a stenciled image of a maniacally grinning skull wearing a fedora and fur coat, its bony fingers crossed for good luck. Called "Señor Suerte" (Mr. Luck.) the character was undoubtedly part of a long-standing continuum of graffiti that had adorned Los Angeles walls for previous decades, from territorial shoeshine boys to zoot suiters and cholos, but it was also something new. A proclamation of identity and territory for sure, it was accompanied by an artist's signature, but in its reflective power and cultural commentary, it was also undeniably art.

Señor Suerte's creator, a young Latino kid from the surrounding neighborhood named Chaz Bojorquez, would later explain how the image was a deliberate integration of Latino Día de Muertos imagery, blaxploitation films like *Shaft* and *Superfly*, and the emerging hippie scene he had begun to explore (the original version was actually smoking a joint.)

And as Suerte began to appear alongside the freeways and on overpasses, its influence quickly spread. First through the surrounding neighborhood, where it was co-opted by the local Avenues gang on both the streets and in prison where a tattoo of it represented both the neighborhood and a perceived protection from death. "I learned an important lesson from them on the question of 'What is the true value of art?'" Chaz explains. "I feel like when I finish a painting its value is zero. True value comes when someone first believes in the imagery."

But this visionary "gothic cholo" aesthetic would eventually reach much further than just the surrounding neighborhood and its inhabitants—its effect soon apparent in the emerging skate and surf culture of Dogtown, then in the raucous punk rock scene in Hollywood, and eventually, decades later, in a newly christened "street art" movement.

***

More than forty years later, Chaz Bojorquez, on a rare break from painting, gazes across the hills of Northeast Los Angeles. The neighborhood below, a dense collection of small houses and circuitous streets called Highland Park, is where he grew up, and where, in the late sixties, he established himself as one of the preeminent graffiti artists. He still lives there today. For so many decades the area has been a predominantly working-class Latino community, home to both an esteemed college and the notorious Avenues street gang. But like so much of urban America, it is all currently in flux. Modest homes are being sold and quickly resurrected as more expensive dwellings. The small family-owned businesses along the boulevard giving way to tonier restaurants and boutiques, and all of it occurring at an almost unimaginable pace. Asked what he thinks about it all, Chaz smiles and says simply, "LA is a city of change." Then after a beat, adds, "But I feel for the people who get driven out. That could be my family."

Few visual artists have so powerfully and personally captured the feel of life in Los Angeles. Not the perception of it, but the actual reality of it with all the maddening contradictions—the architectural ugliness and natural beauty, the unseen communities, a pervasive sense of isolation, sporadic violence, and the inimitable coolness and style. And really, who better to document all of this than Chaz, who has lived so much of it?

While it's true that he was prowling the freeway overpasses and riverbeds at night, writing his name and throwing up prototypical street art, Chaz also continued to educate himself and augment his considerable skillset. During those early years, he was also taking classes in calligraphy, studying Asian brush techniques, and attending classes taught by a lettering artist in Hollywood. As he later explains, "The idea came to me that I could also use it to write cholo graffiti. So, I applied everything I learned from Asian brush philosophy to enhance the meaning of the paint strokes in my own work." Unlike many street artists, Chaz eschews spray paint, choosing to instead render his letters with meticulous brush strokes. "I'm old enough that I saw the first spray can come in around 1953," he explains. "The early spray cans had no pressure and no pigment and would dribble and spit. So I used the chisel brush. With the straight edge, I could do a thin line or thick line."

And while he blasted Señor Suerte around the neighborhood, Chaz also attended the prestigious Chouinard Art Institute that would eventually morph into what is now Cal Arts. "When I went to art school, I met these other guys that were really interested in graffiti but only as an artistic endeavor because they were not Latino," he says. "For them, it was just a fun thing to do during the summer and then they quit. But I continued because I had found a sense of identity. I was very uncomfortable with who I was and where I fit in, and doing graffiti empowered me.

***

In the following years, Chaz existed as sort of a lone wolf. Having seen the the murals of Chicano artists Willie Herron and Magú (aka Gilbert Lujan) Chaz ventured to East LA's renowned Self Help Graphics, where beloved founder Sister Karen, politely proclaimed his work "gutter art" "That was the time of Cesar Chavez," Chaz says. "And they thought the gangster stuff would undermine everything they were saying. They didn't see the art of it. They went academic on me."

Yet he persevered, a solitary force moving through the city, painting walls for reasons entirely his own. He had no crew, no gallery, nobody was watching. And in that inadvertent freedom, Chaz continued to evolve and perfect his art. He studied typefaces like Old English, the lettering many Chicano writers used to instill their words with a sense of pride and almost religious importance. "I was interested in knowing more about graffiti," he says. "So I studied the typefaces. How Old English came from the Gutenberg press and was the typeface of the hierarchy that only they could read, the letter of the church and the bible, that was on your birth and death certificate. I also thought about graffiti grammar and punctuation. Nobody had thought about what those symbols meant."

He also found influences in surf and hippie culture, in particular the work of cartoonist Rick Griffin whose iconic concert posters for legendary San Francisco venue The Fillmore (Jimi Hendrix, Grateful Dead, etc.) added the element of dimensional drop shadows to Old English lettering.

For years, Chaz spent his day working in advertising, designing billboards, and working in Hollywood creating logos for films such as The Warriors and Turk 182, and titles for The Empire Strikes Back, the Muppet movies and James Bond. As well as supporting himself, Chaz also studied and integrated these skills into his art. "I saw my work as signage that you drive by on the freeway," he explains. "I wanted to make sure that it was clear who I was. So, I knew what size of image I wanted, what size of letters, I knew that you had three seconds to see the image and get all the information. And so, I worked over and over again to make it perfect. It wasn't just a tag. I was creating a symbol that was polished. Not to be famous, not to make money, but because it was cool, and it was my trip. I don't know why, but it became really important to me."

***

In the early eighties, talented New York street artists like Keith Haring, Jean-Michel Basquiat and others began to attract serious attention (and dollars) from a newly smitten East Coast art world. Los Angeles remained decidedly out of the spotlight. Local galleries, located primarily on the wealthier west side, focused primarily on established artists, all but ignoring a thriving and anarchistic scene flourishing in gritty Hollywood and downtown. For most underground artists on the West Coast, the choice was move to New York or, like Chaz, work a Hollywood adjacent day job that managed to utilize one's talents.

And in the absence of any real attention, a unique underground scene began to thrive in Los Angeles, merging subcultures and styles in a way that would eventually influence the look of the world. "Nobody knew what we were doing out here," Chaz says. "Everybody left us alone and that was our strength. We had our own punk scene and the punks would show up with cholo headbands in a low rider and then go surfing, and it would all be the same person."

It was during this time that Chaz found an artistic home and community at the Zero One Gallery in Hollywood. Founded by John Pochna and Wayzata de Camerone, it served as both an illegal after-hours drinking establishment and art gallery for an eclectic clientele ranging from local punk bands to John Belushi. There, Chaz met self-proclaimed "lowbrow" artists like Robert Williams and Big Daddy Roth and others, like recently departed printmaker Richard Duardo and the late Mike Kelly. The scene was influenced by a mix of cultures including underground comics, punk rock, hotrods, and surfing. It was at the Zero One that Chaz got his first of several solo shows. It would also prove the beginning of an unlikely movement of worldwide consequence.

"We were all hanging around Zero One and people are starting to die from alcoholism and car crashes," Chaz remembers. "We would be having these wakes at the gallery for friends, because nobody cared about our work, and we were there drinking. I was complaining that nobody loved graffiti, nobody loved cartoons, what are we gonna do, and then I said, we've gotta do what the Chicanos do, we've got to self-validate. So Greg Escalante and Robert Williams decided we needed our own magazine and, with some other guys (Craig Stecyk, *Thrasher* magazine's Fausto Vitello) they created *Juxtapoz*."

The late Escalante was a fan and believed that Chaz would ultimately prove more influential than any established East Coast street art stars. "The chapter on Chaz is not closed and he is working hard every day on his art," he explained. "I believe that, when the chapter is finally written in its entirety, Chaz will be seen as a worldwide seminal figure in the art world, whose love for and choice of graffiti will have a profound and lasting effect on our culture."

***

In recent years Chaz has taken to incorporating different types of text into his work. More than just names, but poetry, visually and literally. Along with manipulating type size and placement to create a sense of visual rhythm, he has been using lines of actual poetry. Several newer works feature the words of a 13th-century Persian poet named Jalaluddin Rumi.

"Everything that he wrote was about drinking and parties and being free with women and enjoying life," Chaz explains. "One line is, 'We come spinning out of nothingness, scattering stars like dust.' And I have that in a painting, scattering stars, is like doing graffiti to me. Another line of his I use is, 'I desire drunken parties and wild dance.'" Chaz has also been using his own words as well, an example being "If the city was a body, graffiti would show you where it hurts" and another being "Any drawn line that speaks about identity and unity and dignity, that line is art."

While Chaz is without a doubt, one of the premier graffiti artists, he is more than that. It would be inaccurate to characterize him as a single thing, be it Chicano artist, graffiti artist, or fine art painter, because, in reality, he is all of that at once. It is a deliberate defying of categorization that has perhaps, in the short term, made him more difficult to market, but will likely allow his work to have a far more lasting effect. To date, Chaz has works in collections at The Smithsonian, LA County Museum of Art, Los Angeles Museum of Contemporary Art, and more, while his works have been exhibited in cities throughout the world including Paris, Madrid, Tokyo, Berlin, Rome, and Mexico City.

The oldest known art, found in the caves of Indonesia, dates back 39,900 years. It is merely a stencil of a human hand pressed against a rock wall. As if whoever created it yearned to prove their very existence, to tell others, in the coming days and years, simply that they had been there, been alive in that very place. And to a large extent, that is what all art is. A document of who we are in certain moments, what we are thinking and feeling, what the world around us looked like. Chaz Bojorquez does just that. He is an artist who powerfully and skillfully captures the world around him as he has experienced it. With placement of paint and text, he documents the lives of his friends, family, and neighborhood, and what it means to live in Los Angeles.

"When I was young, we traveled the riverbed at night and called it the diamond-studded highway," he says. "Generations of broken bottles glistened in the moonlight. The riverbed's concrete walls gave us a canvas that stretched for miles. It paralleled the freeway and the car lights blinked across the walls, giving them a cinematic look, like film going through a giant projector. Being with twenty friends and painting a mural, having so much fun, those days are over. The freedom of youth is reinvented with every generation, every movement has its time to end and we are no different. Graffiti is about freedom. It's an art form that you don't need permission to do, and I feel just as free now as that dude running around throwing up my first tag so many years ago."

Like the city around him, constantly changing and reinventing itself, Chaz's work continues to evolve in both method and intent. Not satisfied to merely reflect on the feats of his youth and past glories, he is up there in his studio right now, observing this very moment, living it, painting it.

Mickey Avalon's True Hollywood Stories

From the LA Weekly

The blond girl is reaching toward the stage, trying to grab the singer's partially exposed ass as he leans out over the crowd. The tight jeans he's wearing are now strategically torn in the back, and she can see the pale skin just inside. She screams out to him, "Mickey!" But as her manicured fingers near their target, he suddenly reaches down and squeezes her hand, then turns and shimmies off across the stage, raising a bottle of expensive tequila to his mouth and gulping it down like water. The girl falls back into the arms of her friends, smiling beatifically, her glossy lips parting to reveal a set of expensive-looking braces. She can't be a day over 15, and she's obviously wasted. "Mickey…"

Like a young Mick Jagger, the singer is shirtless and skinny, ugly and pretty. He strolls across the stage holding a microphone, then grabs a noticeably drugged-out backup dancer and kisses her on the mouth. He shoves her hard across the stage, and she stumbles in her heels and falls forward onto the floor, legs splayed apart in her short dress, eyes closed the whole time. "Mickey…"

The singer's head dips and bobs to a pounding beat emanating from the club's sound system. His friend, also shirtless, stands next to him, leaning out over the crowd and pouring tequila into opened mouths as if delivering a communion. A large, athletic boy bolts across the stage and tries to tackle the singer before he's dragged off. Raising the microphone to a face adorned with glittery, half-smeared makeup, the singer surveys the scene before him. Screaming girls? Uh-huh. Jealous and sexually confused boys? Sure. Sold-out show at the legendary Roxy? Okay. Is this the beginning of a full-scale glam-rock revival on the Sunset Strip? Despite the heady promise of drugs and debauchery coursing through the young and predominantly white crowd, not exactly.

The singer tosses his longish hair back and begins to *rap*. There's a certain disconnect, yet strangely it works. His voice is a slightly effeminate drawl, teasing out the words…

"Mickey Avalon, dick thick as a baton, the illest motherfucker from here to Vietnam, I used to work nights on hot cock dot com, but then I got fired when my mom logged on. I'm on the run, my dad's a bum, I asked my girl if she loved me and she just said—umm…*"*

Toward the back of the club, two lanky African-American kids are dressed in the uniform of the serious hip-hop aficionado—T-shirts, baggy jeans and tilted baseball caps. They are perched on top of a booth, surveying the scene before them.

"That dude used to be a homosexual prostitute," one of them finally shouts over the loud music.

"For reals?" his friend asks in obvious disbelief.

The first kid just shrugs, and they continue watching.

Backstage after the show, Mickey Avalon strolls into the crowded dressing room like a middleweight champ in mascara and eyeliner. He pours a bucket of ice water over his head and lets out a joyful scream, then pulls two very young-looking groupies close, and the three of them start to kiss and grope one another. A nearby photographer grins and begins to circle around, shooting pictures, while a few feet away, a beautiful girl in a black designer dress kneels down onto the soiled carpet and vomits into a trash can, tears rolling down her cheeks.

"I like a girl who eats and brings it up, a sassy little frassy with bulimia. Her best friend's a plastic surgeon, and when her Beamer's

in the shop she rolls the Benz. Manis and pedis on Sundays and Wednesdays, money from Mommy lovely in Versace. So rich, so pretty, the best piece of ass in the whole damn city."

Mickey Avalon, the world's greatest glam rap star—a genre of one.

I'm sitting with Avalon at a small kitchen table with his grandmother. The décor of her single-story Beverly Hills home seems to have been locked in place sometime during the early 1970s—colorful wallpaper patterns, prickly shag carpet and a minimalist tree painted on the wall behind me. We're here to check some old photos, but when Avalon mentions I'm a writer, his grandmother sits us down and begins to tell her story. It is a harrowing tale for sure—she was a young Jewish woman in Hungary when the Nazis made their move. Avalon is supposed to be heading for a Silver Lake recording studio to lay down some tracks with producer Dave Cooley, but instead, we sit and listen. As she speaks to us in her thick Bela Lugosi accent, I find myself staring at the numbers tattooed onto her forearm.

The ordinary details are the most unsettling. Watching the beloved family dog running desperately after the train as the family is hauled away. Josef Mengele casually sorting the new arrivals at the gates of Auschwitz, separating mother and daughter forever. Her handsome young husband, Avalon's grandfather, a respected and beloved dignitary, was at Auschwitz as well. He's in pictures throughout the house and looks like a movie star in tailored suits and a perfectly tilted fedora. The two of them managed to survive the Final Solution, though not entirely unscathed. The suave grandfather was used in one of Mengele's medical experiments, which left half his body partially paralyzed for many months afterward. The grandmother was severely mauled by the attack dog of Amon Goeth, the sadistic officer portrayed by Ralph Fiennes in the film *Schindler's List*. The rest of the family was extinguished.

Avalon tells me that his father got the words that adorned the gates of Auschwitz, "*Arbeit Macht Frei*" ("Work Makes One Free"), tattooed in bold letters on his forearm, yet the more I learn, the more convinced I am that no one in the family would ever seem that free. It's as if the Holocaust has been imprinted in their DNA, continuing its path of destruction from the children to the grandchildren, even here amid the warm California sunshine.

A week later I drive into the Hollywood Hills, to the home of actor Simon Rex. Walking up a covered stairway leading to the front door, a silhouette with a huge Afro passes by and mumbles, "I'm Rainbow…" Inside, I find Avalon and Rex on the couch, smoking a joint. It was Rex who started Avalon's musical career, three years ago. The two had been introduced through an old friend of Avalon's named Ben, a part-time male model turned career criminal and convict who knew Rex from Rex's own stint in the modeling world.

Rex was originally a stoner from Oakland who drove a forklift. At 18, he met a girl at a rave and, days later, moved to Los Angeles with her and her child so she could pursue a supposed "modeling" career. Desperate times ensued, with both of them doing the occasional modeling gig to pay the rent, some with clothing and some decidedly without. Rex eventually traveled to New York for some legit modeling jobs and was picked to become an MTV VJ. When that job ended (not, as widely rumored, because of his prior appearance in a couple of skin flicks), he moved back to L.A., where he has appeared in several films and sitcoms. Despite his photogenic good looks, Rex comes across in person more borscht-belt comic than a *TRL* video shill. On his friendship with Avalon, he explains, "We're really just two neurotic Jews. You should hear us try and decide where to have breakfast. Half the time we just give up."

To occupy the downtime between acting gigs, longtime hip-hop fan Rex had purchased a home recording system and set about "making beats." His songs, which he performs under the moniker "Dirt Nasty," tend to be lewd, satirical raps about the Hollywood scene he has come to inhabit. On his most popular song to date, "Dropping Names," the actor raps about his sometimes real and sometimes imagined dalliances with various starlets. *"I'm hungry for beaver. Give me a call, Sigourney Weaver."*

Avalon was destitute and living on Rex's couch when it all began. He had embraced hip-hop culture since childhood, writing rhymes and doing graffiti with the Russian, Hispanic, and Jewish kids from his West Hollywood neighborhood. At Rex's urging, Avalon started composing his own songs, and the words flowed easily. He eventually made an abbreviated and admittedly self-conscious performance debut alongside Rex on an episode of the MTV show *Cribs*. "At first it was really just two people on drugs fucking around," Avalon says. But when their songs began to improve, Rex started burning CDs and passing them out at the trendy clubs he frequented.

While Rex's humorous lyrics generated the intended laughs, it was Avalon's outrageous and reportedly autobiographical lyrics of bisexual street hustling and narcotics that created a more serious buzz among the moneyed kids who liked to party in Hollywood. And it was these kids' fascination that initially attracted the attention of an aspiring manager (and established club DJ) named Kev E. Kev, whose idea it was to wrap the CDs in pages from the *L.A. Xpress* newspaper, which features lurid advertisements for local dominatrixes, rub-'n'-tug masseuses and escorts.

Thus, the legend of "Mickey Avalon" (not his real name) was born, yet the question lingers—is all this talk of sex, death, and addiction merely calculated Alice Cooper–like theatrics, or is it truly the skinny, white Hollywood version of the 50 Cent/Slick Rick paradigm of turning pain and hardship into art and money?

Mickey Avalon's mother tells me she didn't know his father was a heroin addict when they met, back in the early '70s. We're sitting in a health-food-store café outside of Los Angeles. She is an attractive and surprisingly youthful-looking woman. She says they were just two Jewish teenagers from the Fairfax District, and she couldn't even have imagined somebody using a drug like heroin at the time. Avalon's father was tall and handsome, with an obsessive love for rhythm & blues music. While his peers were embracing flower power and grooving to the Byrds and the Kaleidoscope up in Griffith Park, he was appearing on local TV dance shows in an electric-blue suit, shimmying to the more carnal sounds of Wilson Pickett and James Brown.

They spent the first years of their marriage like many of their generation, trekking through exotic locales like Katmandu, Afghanistan, and Iran, smoking hash and meditating with Buddhist monks. It wasn't until the couple settled back in Los Angeles that things took a turn for the worse. The father became a chiropractor, and they had two children—Mickey and a younger sister. But the father's blossoming heroin addiction proved too much, and the couple soon divorced. "He eventually spiraled out of control, and it wasn't safe anymore, mainly because of the people he was associating with."

Avalon's aunt later tells me it was when his father started hanging out with some "greaser" types, young Vietnam vets from nearby towns like Fontana and Covina, that he started getting into downers and then heroin. She says her brother had always considered himself a poet and was attracted to the darker places, something she theorizes might have been a result of near-constant exposure to their parents' Holocaust experience. Addicted and on his own, Avalon's father quickly descended into the seamier underside of L.A. life.

It was for that reason, the mother says, that she moved herself and her two young children to within the Beverly Hills city limits. "Back then, L.A. County had a reputation that if you had trouble, you would be dead before the police ever arrived," she says. "That wasn't true in Beverly Hills. His father was hanging out with some very dangerous characters back then. Do you remember the Wonderland murders in Laurel Canyon with Eddie Nash and his crew?" (Porn star John Holmes snitched, and four people were brutally beaten to death with lead pipes.) She goes on to tell me that the father's chiropractic practice had evolved into an insurance scam involving Nash's crime syndicate and the RTD (Rapid Transit District). After the divorce, she got word through the grapevine that some of Nash's henchmen had volunteered to knock her off. "They offered to take me out as a favor to him," she explains, "and with those people, that was serious."

By the time Mickey Avalon was 16, he was living on his own. An aspiring painter and part of a well-known Hollywood graffiti crew, he supported himself working for his mother in what the aunt refers to cryptically as "the biz." I have heard several innuendoes about "the biz," yet sitting with his mother over an organic salad, I have a hard time asking about it. As we're about to leave, I finally chance a question. "So what exactly were you doing to make money back then?" She stares at me for a beat, her eyes narrowing, and then nods. Her voice is suddenly less June Cleaver and all business.

"Okay, let me tell you how it was," she says. "It was really hard for a single mother to make it in Los Angeles. My husband's family raised my rent, and he wouldn't give me anything. I was on welfare before that, and then I had two kids in Beverly Hills to support, so I made a living on the black market selling pot. Have you seen that television show, *Weeds*? Well, that's how it was. I didn't tell Mickey about it until I caught him selling his own pot in front of our house. Then I had to sit him down."

Avalon was 14 at the time, and from that point on, he was part of "the biz." They both tell the same story—his mom showed him the best weed he had ever seen, then asked how much he was smoking and how much money he needed a week. He learned the trade well and eventually became one of "the biz's" biggest moneymakers, moving out of the house and into his own apartment.

"She told me how to do it, and I was good at it," he tells me later. "She said, 'If you live outside the law, you got to be totally honest. And your car always has to be perfect. No broken headlights.'" He suddenly becomes a little protective. "She was still a good person," he cautions. "I think she would rationalize it as a means to an end for me. So I could keep painting and pay the rent. She never wanted me to end up the way I did."

It wasn't until his late teens, when Avalon's mom noticed blood on his arms and the all-too-familiar fuzziness of heroin intoxication, that she fired him.

"I just had too much to lose," she explains, sipping herbal tea. "I had worked so hard to achieve a certain lifestyle, and then he was going to throw it all in the toilet because he was on heroin. You can't trust somebody on heroin. You would never pick somebody like that to be on your team. He was making good money and would have made a great partner, but I just saw too much of his dad in him when he was like that."

It's raining hard as I navigate through Hollywood with Avalon and Rex in my car. They had planned to hit a particular strip club to "scout dancers" for an upcoming show, but the establishment has inexplicably closed down, so instead we're heading for a nightclub to check out the scene. The two of them are already high and plan on drinking, so we're rolling my undeniably sensible station wagon as we pull up to the valet stand and disembark among the beautiful people.

Because of Rex's celebrity status and Avalon's emerging notoriety, we are able to breeze past the line and are quickly ushered into a simultaneously sleazy and lavish nightclub. A DJ is spinning a set of oddly disconnected greatest hits, while Amazonian waitresses in tight hot pants cut through the crowd with illuminated bottles of expensive champagne. The girls hanging around the dance floor are, for the most part, young, pretty, and overtly sexy—lots of blond hair, ultratight jeans, miniskirts, and bare midriffs. The guys seem a cross between the neo-Guido, hair-gel-encrusted *Growing Up Gotti* kids and horny junior talent agents. Avalon assures me that anonymous sex in bathroom stalls is not at all uncommon.

Several girls pass by, recognize Rex, and exchange knowing looks. Avalon tells me that even a periodically employed actor rates far higher in the pecking order than most of those in attendance, who have yet to achieve even a small modicum of fame. It also doesn't hurt that Rex has been publicly linked to several high-profile party girls, including the scene's high priestess, Paris Hilton.

Avalon seems a less natural fit for the surroundings—he is neither tan nor rich, and far too grimy for the status-conscious, designer-label crowd. Yet, somehow he has emerged as an unintentional troubadour for the hedonistic scene, and, while admittedly glad for the newfound attention, he remains somewhat of a tourist.

"It's really because of Simon that I've even been able to infiltrate this world," he explains. "I'm still pretty much an outsider. I have a song called 'So Rich So Pretty' that has become a theme song for a lot of these Newport and Malibu girls. They tell me, 'That's just like me.' But it's really a song about how hollow all of it is. How it's just this coked-out scene where all the girls are anorexic. But then, I suppose I'm making fun of myself, too. Because I'm saying that, and then I'm hanging out here and rubbing shoulders with it all."

Later, I'm standing off to the side with Avalon, watching a skinny blond girl do a strange herky-jerky drug dance, when Rex arrives with actor Kevin Connelly, from the hit HBO show *Entourage*, who smiles and tells Avalon he is a fan. He says he recently bought his CD and brought it home to his girlfriend, Nicky Hilton, who told him that she was already totally into Mickey Avalon.

When they head off, Avalon tells me that Paris Hilton recently had him on an episode of her reality show *The Simple Life*. Both Hilton and co-host Nicole Richie were supposed to plan a wedding, and Hilton chose Avalon as the musical entertainment for hers. It turned out to be two girls getting married, and Avalon serenaded them with a song called "Friends and Lovers," about murder and suicide. He says he and his pal Rainbow got so loaded during the shoot that they crashed into a production truck and fled the scene afterward. As we prepare to leave, Rex comes back and says Connelly mentioned having the two of them appear on an episode of *Entourage* as themselves, which seems—perfect.

In his late teens, Avalon was an Orthodox Jew. He grew a beard, wore the black hat, and started attending the strictest temples he could find around West Hollywood, voraciously reading the texts and intensely debating the rabbis.

"Looking back, I was a zealot," he admits. "I didn't grow up very religious, so it actually felt pretty rebellious at the time."

The conversion, he says, was motivated by a belief that he was doomed to end up like his father and that God might be able to save him. His dad was already sick by then, his body breaking down after years of heroin and methadone and a particularly devastating crack run. His teeth were gone, and his legs were painfully swollen from hepatitis and tuberculosis. Avalon was trying to get him into long-term treatment. Avalon's ex-wife was living with them at the time, and when we meet for coffee, she recalls his desperation.

"Their relationship was really reversed at that point," she says. "It was like Mickey was the father and his father was a child. The rehabs wouldn't take his dad until he had been clean for a month, even though he could hardly walk. Mickey literally turned the doorknobs around and locked his dad in so he couldn't go out and buy drugs."

His dad eventually entered treatment and surprised everyone by staying. He was in for a year and emerged clean, if not physically restored. Afterward, he began attending 12-step meetings and forging a new identity, adjusting to life without narcotics.

"He realized he could still be cool without using drugs," Avalon's ex says. "One night, we started talking, and he said I must hate him for what he did to his children. I could tell he felt all this intense guilt, and he broke down and started crying."

Six months after leaving treatment, Avalon's father remained off drugs. Then, almost like the punch line to a cruel cosmic joke, he was leaving an AA meeting one night and was hit by a drunken driver while crossing La Cienega Boulevard. He was taken to the hospital, but a liver destroyed by decades of abuse and disease proved unable to process the infections, and his eyes turned yellow. He never fully regained consciousness. Doctors eventually approached a then-19-year-old Avalon for consent to turn off his father's life support.

"I remember Mickey and his little sister were in the room," Avalon's ex tells me. "And the doctors told us, 'That's it,' and his father just stopped breathing. Mickey just seemed so calm."

When asked about it, Avalon is initially fatalistic about his father's death, saying, "He was sick, and we knew he was never going to live that long. Death don't really faze me much."

Later, though, as we drive through the West Hollywood neighborhood where the two grew up, he softens. "Just because my dad was a junkie didn't mean we didn't go to baseball-card conventions and he didn't turn me on to Marlon Brando movies. We still had all those moments. And I miss him. Not on Father's Day, but right now. I mean, who can I call, all excited, to say, 'Yo, I'm going to be in the *L.A. Weekly*?' Not my dad. He doesn't even know I ever wrote a song."

Both Avalon and his sister had toyed with heroin in their mid-teens, but their father's death appears to have accelerated an ingrained yen for the drug. Avalon attempted to curtail this seemingly inevitable path to self-destruction in the same way his father had, by starting a family. A year after his father's death, Avalon and his teenage bride had a daughter. "It was like my dad took his last breath, and a year later, my daughter let out the loudest scream you have ever heard," he says.

The three of them moved away to Portland to start anew. He had become increasingly disillusioned with the rigid laws of Orthodox Judaism and shaved off his beard the day his daughter came home from the hospital. But as with his father, a family wasn't enough to check Avalon's own descent. He had been smoking and selling pot while attending the Orthodox temples back in Hollywood (there is technically no rule against it, he says) and began using heroin more and more as they settled in Portland, eventually abandoning his wife and daughter altogether for the drug.

Then, at perhaps his lowest point, addicted and living amid the hustlers and street urchins of downtown Portland, and selling his body to support his habit, Avalon called his mom back in Los Angeles to say hello. She told him to come home and says she was genuinely surprised when he called a day later from the downtown L.A. bus station. He moved into his mother's home and managed to kick his drug habit.

Everyone I've heard describe Avalon's younger sister, says that she could light up a room, and that when she spiraled downward, it was with a stunning and frightening intensity.

"She was just like a light," says Avalon's mother. "So charming and beautiful, but she could go to those lower depths just like her father. Mickey would be homeless at a friend's house in Malibu. People take care of him because he doesn't take up much space. And he would never let anybody consciously hurt him. I can't say the same about her. She would be down in MacArthur Park."

Inspired by Avalon's unexpected success, the family managed to track down his sister and bring her home as well. "I thought it would all work out, that we would do it with love," his mother tells me sadly.

"That was the best year of my life," Avalon says without hesitation. "It was the closest I had ever been to my sister, and we were both in my mom's house, which we had left before we were supposed to. It's as if we created and recreated memories during that time."

He says the two of them managed to stay clean as a team, riding the newly constructed subways and trains throughout the city to 12-step meetings. His sister actually slapped him once in public when he started dating a girl, fearful that he was going to abandon her. Then she started dating an older lawyer, who treated her well, and by all accounts, it seemed the unlikeliest of happy endings. But that perfect year ended abruptly one morning when Avalon knocked on his sister's bedroom door. She didn't respond, so he turned the stereo up and headed into the shower. He remembers hearing his mom yelling at his sister, and he shouted for them to stop arguing. It was only when he walked back into the hall that he realized his mom was actually screaming. He looked into his sister's room and saw her sprawled across the bed, her skin pale and blue. Avalon says he looked away, remembering a Jewish tradition that advises one not to view the dead so you might remember them as they were, alive and happy.

"All my friends and all my lovers are dead. Some from cheap narcotics and others from—lead. The filthy rich and the dirt, dirt poor are all the same when they can't take no more, because all my friends and all my lovers are dead."

Late night at Canter's Delicatessen on Fairfax. Avalon is sitting across from me eating a plate of corned beef and cabbage—explaining how exactly he ended up as a male prostitute. It was after his mom fired him from "the biz." He was separated from his wife and child, addicted to heroin, and living in a cheap Portland rooming house. Nearby was a gritty stretch of Jefferson Avenue nicknamed "Vaseline Alley" for obvious reasons. Avalon met a kid while spending the night in jail, and when they were released, he watched the kid make money. When he first tried it, Avalon says, he was just ripping off the "johns"—climbing into the cars and then jumping out with their money.

"But as you get more fucked up, it gets more difficult," he explains. "When you're dealing with $40 tricks on their lunch break, well, that's easy. But when you're dealing with $10 crackheads who take all their clothes off when they take a hit and you're locked in the motel room, that's when the ball ain't in your court."

He looks across the restaurant, notices a pretty blond girl a few booths over and waves to her. She smiles and waves back. He tells me she's a girl from the neighborhood and they went to high school together. He sifts through the cabbage with his fork for a beat and continues.

"It got to be a really dark, weird time. I mean, I've given guys hand jobs, but I've never been fucked in the ass and I've never sucked a guy's dick. I know that to most people anything like that is gay. But I know what I like, so I have no problem, because, at the end of the day, it's just an act. I would much rather give a hand job than wash dishes all day. Does that make me gay? I don't know, I don't think so. It was tragic that I was such a complete loser, but then again, I wasn't exactly supposed to be a lawyer or a stockbroker."

"When you've got some money then come and get your jollies, a corner teen in this California dream, all up on the scene dipped in Vaseline. My foster parents told me that I could be anything I wanted to, so I became me Mickey Avalon, the kid who runs free serving

sucker MCs and getting paid for my delivery. I freak beats that stain your silk sheets, filthy on the mic like Lenny Bruce used to be."

The Mickey Avalon I have come to know is far different from what I expected as I drove to my first meeting with the latest great white hip-hop hope. Intelligent, candid and seemingly without guile, Avalon had his heart on his sleeve from the moment we met. While he talks of death and loss with something resembling calm detachment, there is an undeniable air of vulnerability about him that is both refreshing and, at times, unnerving. Heroin is, after all, a painkiller, and junkies, using or not, tend to feel almost everything. Avalon told me that he is an insomniac, awake throughout the night, painting, reading books and writing. It is not, he says, something he particularly enjoys, those silent hours alone with his thoughts and memories.

Avalon's booked for another sold-out Saturday night show at the Roxy. The previous day, a DJ named Stryker, on the all-powerful KROQ radio station, went on air for several minutes raving about the new underground sensation called Mickey Avalon and how he had done it all on his own. He talked about the Roxy show, and then played Avalon's club hit "Jane Fonda." Saturday morning, there's a message posted on Avalon's MySpace page that reads, "Just to let you know the entire city of Laguna Beach is coming tonight."

When Avalon leaves the sound check on Saturday afternoon, several girls are already gathered outside the club, dressed in vintage aerobics outfits inspired by his "Jane Fonda." They spot Avalon as he starts to walk home and yell out that they love him, which he likes. He makes no bones about wanting success. A true child of Hollywood, fame is really the only currency he has known. Sell enough records and maybe he won't have to go back to delivering pizzas and sleeping on people's couches, might even be able to send his daughter to college when she grows up.

Hours before the show, Avalon is in his West Hollywood apartment, standing in front of a mirror doing his makeup and hair while listening to the sad music of Elmore James. He admits that he rarely, if ever, listens to hip-hop, favoring old rhythm & blues and country music. He's a huge fan of female country singers like Gillian Welsh and Lucinda Williams, and his favorite concert of the past year was Dolly Parton's. It all goes back to his father the record collector. It was the one love he never abandoned and was somehow able to pass down to his son.

"My dad would buy records before paying child support," Avalon says with a laugh. The snub was perhaps lightened when Avalon inherited his dad's prized collection, which he has managed to hold on to over the years.

Avalon emerges from the bathroom in tight jeans, glittering red lipstick, and powder-blue eye shadow. There is an Ace bandage coated with fake blood wrapped across his midsection, and he puts on a silvery Ziggy Stardust–style leather jacket with red, lightning-bolt lapels. The phrase "Thank You" is tattooed across his stomach in bold letters.

"I got that at a time I was having sex with a lot of beautiful girls and I was *really* grateful," he explains with a smile. He also has the phrase "I'm sorry" tattooed on the palm of his hand and the word "Please" etched onto the inside of his bottom lip.

Steve Lindsey, a record producer who worked with the likes of Leonard Cohen and Elton John before forming his own publishing company, recently signed Avalon to a publishing deal. So far, Lindsey's stable of writers has penned such hits as "In Da Club" for 50 Cent, "The Real Slim Shady" for Eminem and "Breakaway" for Kelly Clarkson. He later tells me he rarely signs artists but made an exception with Avalon. While he likes the songs, it was the live show that really hooked him.

"It's David Bowie," Lindsey says. "I think Mickey Avalon's going to bring that kind of entertainment back to rock & roll."

When I ask if he thinks Middle America is ready for Avalon's decidedly ambisexual imagery, he laughs. "Will Middle America be totally aghast? Well, I hope so, or how are we going to make any money? He has the skateboard kids and the young Hollywood crowd out here, but in Middle America, I think he'll get the sexually confused kids, like what happened with Alice Cooper and Bowie."

Standing in his apartment, Avalon checks his reflection one last time, then twists open a bottle of expensive tequila and takes a pull. He slips on a trench coat and announces he is ready.

The sidewalk in front of the Roxy is swarming with kids. The club was selected for historical significance, having hosted such luminaries as Lou Reed, David Bowie, and Prince, but also because it is an all-ages venue, allowing for Avalon's growing legion of teenage fans. We park up the street and navigate across Sunset to the Shamrock Social Club, a tattoo parlor run by renowned tattoo artist Mark Mahoney. Mahoney is a tall, impeccably dressed Bostonian with slicked-back hair and piercing eyes. He was a friend of Avalon's dad and, over the years, developed into one of Avalon's many surrogate father figures throughout the city.

"I lost most of my family unit, so I'll adopt anyone if they work out for me," Avalon explains. Mahoney seems truly glad to see Avalon walk through the door, and even happier when he notes that his pupils are a normal size. Avalon tells him he's staying off the dope, and Mahoney smiles, saying, "Hey, that's fucking great."

He is obviously happy for Avalon's success but says he has no interest in seeing the show, explaining, "My wife and the guys from the shop go see him and come back and tell me stories about what it's like. I know it's all about debauchery and he plays up the effeminate-hustler thing. I don't think it would shock me if he wasn't like one of my kids."

Across the street, we hit the Roxy's side entrance, and some young girls recognize him and begin yelling out to him, "Mickey! Mickey!" We make a beeline through the packed club, up the stairs, and into the backstage area. Unlike at the previous gig, there is no raucous party in the dressing room this time. Avalon has a new stage show, including dancers and several costume changes, so the area has been intentionally cleared. Avalon is now wired and antsy, pacing back and forth and announcing to no one in particular: "Let's go; I want to do this right now."

I head downstairs and find a vantage point toward the back of the club. A contingent of professional surfers from the RVCA clothing team, which sponsors Avalon and recently took him to Japan for a performance, are there, making the scene and drinking everything in sight. Some members of Avalon's old tagging crew, CBS (Can't Be Stopped), are there as well, one tall gent explaining, "He's an old friend and we take care of one another. And he's an entertainer, so he might say or do something someone doesn't like. We like to be around in case people get the wrong idea." A well-dressed Russian next to him nods in silent agreement.

Minutes later, the houselights dim and Avalon's theme music starts —a mix of Tony Basil's "Mickey" and Roxy Music's "Avalon." The curtain slowly rises to reveal a bed with pink satin sheets, fluffy pillows, and teddy bears. There are two fashion-model-like girls frolicking on the bed in nightgowns. Suddenly Avalon appears, creeping through a large stage window, wearing a mask and shining a flashlight on them. The girls act scared and scatter, as a song starts up with a sample of a man's voice announcing, *"We are going to have open sexual intercourse on every street corner of America."* A loud cheer erupts, and Avalon launches into his song "Waiting to Die," soon joined onstage by the two scantily clad girls, who now dance beside him like a sexed-up version of Dean Martin's Golddiggers. The audience is singing along with him.

"Mickey Avalon—the kosher salami. For 20 you get Chachi but 40 gets you Fonzie. A motherfuckin' hustler kamikaze, I used to bus tables but now I sell my body. It's like a jungle, sometimes it makes me wonder, that God must be one sick motherfucker."

Between songs, the young girls down front begin to chant his name, "Mi-ckey! Mi-ckey!," like he's a bona fide David Cassidy–style pop star. A few songs in, someone points out Santino, from last season's reality hit *Project Runway*, pumping his fist and singing along. In front of me is a group of kids who can't be much more than 10 or 11, and they are singing along as well. *"Ty was a stripper, died on the shitter with a smile on her face and her hand on her liver, but I ain't mad, I forgive her, I just get a little sad every time I fuck her sister."* A 30-ish woman I assume to be a mother eventually turns to the kids and says, "He's the Antichrist." The kids smile and keep singing. At one point between songs, Avalon tells the crowd, "You could all be home watching Pearl Jam on *Saturday Night Live*, but you're here with me and I love you all." During the next song, he walks along the front of the stage and kisses all the girls.

When he eventually does an encore, Avalon brings his longtime friend Armin, a.k.a. rapper Andre Legacy, and Simon Rex up onstage. The two of them are dressed like Jesus Christ, while Avalon is now wearing a short tutu. As the crowd screams and cheers for Avalon, it suddenly occurs to me that maybe this isn't merely some hedonistic freak show but a celebration. Perhaps what these kids are responding to, even rejoicing in, is Avalon's unfaltering bravado. This is someone who had to pull the plug on his drug-addicted father, discovered his little sister dead, and jerked off creeps for drug money. Yet, there he is, up onstage, feeling sexy and confident and laughing about it all—and there's something inspiring, even heroic, about that. Hate him or love him, Mickey Avalon is what all stars really are—

reflective light.

After the show, Avalon stands on Sunset Boulevard surrounded by fawning young girls, like some tattered hustler prince. The owner of the club looks on and tells me, "We love him. He's on his way now." A photographer's flashbulb begins to illuminate the street, while an exhausted, but obviously happy, Avalon poses under the marquee with his name proclaiming the show sold out. Minutes later, as I'm driving home through Hollywood, I recall what the tattooist Mark Mahoney said when I asked his thoughts on Avalon's strange and sometimes tragic life. He just shook his head and, in a near whisper, said, "It's just an unbelievable dope opera."

"What to do when your luck is through, whether you come from the slums or live in Malibu. See him running down the avenue, Mickey Avalon with an attitude."

Hardball

From the LA Weekly

It's 107 degrees and I'm standing on the dying grass of a San Fernando Valley baseball field. The uniform I'm wearing isn't helping the situation. It's made of some nonorganic semi-stretchy material that seems to both absorb and seal in the summer heat, turning me into a smoldering, fly-ball-fearing, human Jiffy Pop with a baseball hat on my head.

I look over at the dugout and see my dog, Wally, trying to dig her way out of the heat. Little Italian Alex sees me and smiles, shrugs, as my pooch kicks up a steady barrage of dirt in her quest for subterranean cool. Not a bad move, I think. If I had a shovel out here I might do the same. But of course, the minute I finished, some bastard would likely pound a fly ball into right field. I'd have just enough time to stumble out into the sunlight, raise my glove skyward and watch with horror as the ball plopped to the grass beside me.

That, of course, is the curse of the outfielder: long stretches that lull you into believing you're a mere spectator, punctuated by sudden events with the potential to eradicate all self-esteem. I begin to pace in nervous circles, pounding a fist into my 1974 Davey Lopesmodel glove.

Over at third base, Johnny keeps touching the brim of his hat and shifting from foot to foot. It could be the volatility of third base, where a line drive can suddenly scream toward you at upward of 100 miles an hour. Then again, it could be the gambling habit that keeps Johnny out at various Eastside card palaces till the early a.m. It could also be the love life that makes his tidy one-bedroom seem like a personally funded halfway house for wayward strippers and prostitutes. Either way, he's on edge, and that's a good thing at third base.

I refocus on the infield and see that play has momentarily stopped. Our tattooed, *Mean Streets* worshipping catcher, Dino, has pulled off his mask and is marching out to the mound to confer with our freshly immigrated Japanese pitcher, Masashi. I once asked Masashi what pearls of wisdom old Dino gave him in such situations. He grinned and told me, “He said to think of a blowjob.”

Dino is the ex-drummer of a band called the Hangmen. He borders on having Tourette's syndrome and is prone to sudden eruptions of profanity, mostly directed toward the league's umpires, who he believes have established a far-reaching conspiracy to systematically lower his batting average. He also takes great joy in loudly sharing the sordid details of his latest sexual adventures, which usually involve women's unwashed feet or socks. But Dino's enthusiasm for self-expression is by no means limited to mere verbal outbursts. When it appears he might strike out at bat, the rest of us desperately scramble for cover, knowing if a third strike is called, an aluminum bat will soon be sailing through the air toward the bench. Nothing personal on Dino's part. He just doesn't like letting the team down.

With Dino crouched behind home plate, Masashi leans back and hurls a searing fastball. By the time the batter can swing, the ball is already cooling in Dino's mitt and the inning is over. Masashi heads for the dugout, smiling demurely as the rest of us sing his name. It's all part of his “American” experience. It's all part of mine, too. This is amateur baseball in Los Angeles.

***

So how did someone like me, an ex-punk-rock narcotic waste disposal turned espresso-drinking closet intellectual in his 30s, end up standing out here in a cheap baseball uniform? And why am I caring with all my heart whether my team can somehow avoid self-destructing and manage to win this one game? Although we are tied for first place in the league and leading by three runs, lately we have developed this awful tendency to destroy ourselves in a single horrifying inning of jaw-dropping errors, muttered death threats and near-suicidal depression. Perhaps it's just the game of baseball, or maybe it's the fact that the team is made up of ex-junkies, ex-convicts and crazy foreigners. We are an emotional bunch.

This all began with our manager, now pacing the crowded dugout, puffing a cigarette and barking out his latest mantra of hardball enlightenment: "No stupid base running! Be smart out there!" His arm is cradled in a thick plaster cast, and he's looking a bit pale and shaky. It could be the stress of a championship game, but it could also be the cocktail of prescription painkillers he's been knocking back lately. His name is Mike Coulter, and he's the founder of this team called the Griffith Park Pirates.

Back in the late '80s, Mike moved out from Baltimore with an engineering degree and dreams of becoming a rock star. Not surprisingly, he ended up in a one-room Echo Park roach palace, shooting heroin and listening to Nick Cave records.

Mike finally managed to clean up and put together a band. He called his little power trio Lifter and started playing the clubs around Silver Lake. They had a minor college radio hit and were snatched up by Interscope Records. The future looked bright. Lifter's debut was an obsessive sonic diary of Mike's broken heart at the hands of a girl named Melinda. He titled the album, well, *Melinda.* When it failed to generate the massive sales Interscope desired, the company, not unlike Melinda, stopped returning his calls.

Mike took it all surprisingly well. He had tried, and that was all that mattered. Back at his old day job, he began to daydream about baseball and the idea of playing again. Like many a rebellious youth, he had been forced out of the game by a narrow-minded coach back in his hometown. "I was at a Catholic high school and my hair was a little too long," he says.

Three summers ago, I'm standing in an alley playing catch with Mike when he starts ranting about how he's gonna start a team. Says he found a league sponsored by the city. Not some typical sissified softball league for out-of-shape beer guzzlers fielding balls with a chicken wing in one hand. No, sir, this here is the real deal. Baseball. Hardball. At which point I'm thinking two things: Mike might well be loaded and talking out of his ass, but if he's not, how the hell am I going to back out of this without looking like a complete coward?

See, I hadn't played any serious baseball since the tender age of 11. That was the year an older kid who looked amazingly like a young non-albino Johnny Winter sauntered across an empty schoolyard and sold me my first joint. Don't let anyone tell you that you can't get stoned on cat shit and sunflower seeds. And don't let anybody tell you the evil weed doesn't lead to harder drugs.

Sports weren't really an option after that. Next thing I know I'm 15 years old, wearing a black thrift-store suit and playing minimalist guitar in a gothic punk band called Christian Death. My friend Roger is upfront singing in a full wedding gown, and the stage is littered with flowers stolen from the local graveyard. Everyone in my pubescent crowd is staggering around in a narcotic-induced haze, imagining themselves some hybrid of William Burroughs and Jean Genet miraculously transplanted from decadent prewar Berlin into the saccharine suburbs of Southern California. Then, for me, it's a downward spiral of hard drugs, a failed art school attempt, two years playing drums for the punk band Bad Religion, several slumber parties in the county jail, and finally a state-sponsored 18-month stay in a hardcore treatment center.

After 12 years of rebuilding my life, joining Mike Coulter's baseball team makes perfect sense to me. Not so for some of the others in our crowd. When faced with the commitment of actually joining a team, with matching uniforms and schedules, a lot of the guys we know simply vanish. Though they all claim to possess near-legendary baseball skills, when push comes to shove they somehow can't pull the trigger. This is not surprising. The area where most of us live, Silver Lake, is the virtual epicenter of hipster irony. Sincerity is at best ignored and at worst ridiculed. This is a neighborhood that once boasted a well-organized adult kickball game, where Scooby-Doo lunch pails are collected like rare coins. If Mike and I had casually announced we were going to permanently sear the image of, say, Shaun Cassidy into our buns, nobody would have batted an eye. This was different, though. In this endeavor we risked committing the worst of all possible social sins: caring and looking stupid.

***

When I hear that my friend Clay played some high school ball down in Orange County, I begin a persistent recruitment process on par with some fat-cat big-college alum. Three days later we finalize the deal over a cup of *con leche* at the Café Tropical and a promise to help the employment-challenged Clay with his league fees.

At first glance, Clay seems an unlikely prospect: late 30s, tanned arms covered with faded tattoos, face weathered by a hard life, and too much California sunshine. Back in the late '80s, he hooked up with a noisy hard-rock band called Junkyard and signed a big deal with Geffen. At the time, he had amassed a few drug-related legal problems. After formalizing the deal, Clay went to score some celebratory smack, got arrested, and found himself in county jail on a no-bail felony warrant. Geffen obviously saw dollar signs in Junkyard, so it hired a big-shot lawyer, but the best even he could do was get Clay a year. Languishing in his cell, Clay wondered if the band would wait for him. Much to everyone's surprise, they did.

Eight months later our boy hits the street and everything's looking sweet. The album gets great reviews and the video's all over MTV. Clay's living the rock & roll dream. Trouble is, his drug habit is completely out of whack, even for a boozy rock band like Junkyard. Soon he's out of the band, back on the streets and back in jail.

He gets out after another year, tries to clean up, and fails miserably. Finds himself living in a broken-down Continental on Ninth and Pico with some sweaty Polish guy and a growling rottweiler. From there it's an ugly roller-coaster ride of detoxes, jail cells, shit jobs, and blown chances. He finally manages to get off dope, and in 1998 we recruit him to our fledgling baseball team. He ends up fielding line drives at the hot corner, third base.

The team's next signing is a lumbering long-ball hitter named Chris. With the tanned, muscular good looks of an '80s porn star, he's yet another formerly promising high school athlete who saw his future obliterated by a combo of nihilistic punk rock and nasty street drugs. Years later Mike Coulter finds him cleaned up and working a local sound stage, where his addiction has metamorphosed into an all-encompassing need to romance anything with no fur and a heartbeat.

***

As the first season approaches, we're still short a few players. Turns out that the league has a waiting list, and that there are two names on it. We call them both. Whoever they are, they want to play baseball and that's good enough. We sign them up sight unseen, pay our league fees, and are officially a team, the Griffith Park Pirates. We all drive down to East L.A. to purchase our nonorganic, heat-confining uniforms.

Our ace pitcher, Masashi, is one of the names from the list. He's just arrived from Japan with a hunger to play hardball. I figure when he learns enough English to fully comprehend who he's playing with, he'll bow graciously and run screaming for the hills. Until then we'll enjoy his company and his fastball. This particular theory is shot to hell when Masashi arrives for practice in a lime-green cardigan. He walks to the mound and everyone starts clapping. Emblazoned across his back is the huge skull emblem of the New York punk band the Misfits. Needless to say, we all appreciate his daring juxtaposition of classic prep and old-school hardcore. A few weeks later someone spots him diving off the stage at a Rancid concert.

When I sit with Masashi at his favorite noodle shop in Little Tokyo, he tells me how he was following the accepted Japanese career path when he suddenly had a life-changing realization. He saw his future and it looked, well, boring. "My major was civil engineering. But after a half-month in school, I wanted to quit. So boring. And I talked with my grandmother and mother, but they were so freaked out. I said I want to quit university and I want to study acting." He then upped the ante by telling his family that he was headed for Hollywood. Whereupon he packed his bags and just took off. His old friends looked on in stunned politeness. "I was on a path. I jumped off. But my friends couldn't do that."

Masashi landed in L.A. and, like any right-thinking transplant, headed straight for smoggy West Covina. There, surrounded by mini-malls and sun-cracked stucco, he began studying English at some school for oblivious foreigners. After a while, he saw the light and moved into L.A. proper, where he started to study acting. It's at this point that he heads down to the Parks and Recreation office, puts his name on the baseball list, and joins the team.

Soon he's soaking up motivational speeches from Dino. "That's what I was hoping, to get involved with Americans and get to know an unknown world for me. When I'm in the dugout, I'm very proud of our team. I just look at everyone and it is very cool. I am so glad to be in there."

***

The other player on the waiting list is yet another aspiring thespian from a far-off exotic land. His name is Jacob and he comes to us from Appalachian West Virginia. He played junior high baseball back in them there hills until, as with Mike Coulter, the coach objected to his long hair. Jacob did have a few behavioral problems as well. Youthful indiscretions like drinking and joyriding helped land him a short stay in reform school.

Re-enrolled in high school, Jacob fell hard for a teen temptress. So smitten, in fact, that he followed her into the theater department. He ended up in a play that made it all the way to a state drama competition, where he won the award for best-supporting actor. No more joyriding for Jacob—now he wanted to act. After high school he headed west to Oregon, where he pounded the boards of community theater, paying the rent with a series of mind-numbing factory jobs. Several years later, he splits for the bright lights of Hollywood.

"This city is amazing. You can do anything you want here. I mean, any dream," Jacob says. "And baseball is just like a dream." Like Masashi, he finds his way to the park's office and puts his name on the waiting list. A few months later, he gets a call from the Griffith Park Pirates. From day one, Jacob refuses to wash his hat, invoking some backwoods, Burt Reynolds-inspired good-luck ritual. We put him, and his stinky hat, at second base.

***

That first season we take a beating. The other teams have been playing longer and are much younger. Most, if any, haven't spent the last 10 years living out some tribute to a '70s-era Lou Reed. We have our moments, but we lose a lot of games. We are, however, surprised to find out just how much winning matters.

The other thing that surprises me is how much fun we're having. We all show up an hour before game time to warm up and toss the ball around. We actually talk strategy—in the car, on the street, in massage parlors. On holidays we duck out of family get-togethers to meet and practice. It's stunning to see my world-weary comrades playing with such joy. When we actually do win a game, the buzz lasts for days. We decide to sign up and play the winter season.

***

As the second summer approaches, the team gets a few new players. Will is a first-generation Cuban immigrant, and Mike L., a first-generation Basque immigrant. They grew up together as teen punks in Downey, heckling Richard Carpenter—of the Carpenters —as he angrily mowed his parents' lawn.

"It was really fun to be punks in Downey back then," Will smiles fondly. "Cops literally hated us and would chase us down. And men would fight us. You know, we're 13-, 14-year-olds, and like 30-year-old mulletheads with mustaches would pull their Camaros over and fight us. And we would have big gang wars with the 'Hessians,' the metalheads. We would meet behind Bobo's Arcade and have gang fights." Will and Mike now have lots of tattoos and live in Los Angeles. On weekends they play together in a traditionalist three-chord punk band called the Dimwits.

The other new guy is a bit more unconventional. He's about 5 feet tall and rail thin, and dresses entirely in black, resembling a classier, extremely debonair Eddie Munster. When he introduces himself, I have absolutely no idea what language he's speaking, though for some reason he assumes I can understand every word. Turns out his name is Alex, he's Italian, and he's a real-life count. When I ask him about it, he shrugs. "My mother's a countess and I'm a count. We still have a castle and stuff." He thinks Americans tend to romanticize all that "historical shit." To him, a castle is just old and fusty. Other than that he's an average Joe. Well, except for the fact that he's a distant relative of famed boxer Ray "Boom Boom" Mancini.

***

A few games into that second summer, there are some nasty rumors about Clay. They're sadly confirmed when he shows up for a game in long sleeves. The temperature is somewhere near 100 degrees. The following week someone sees him outside his apartment with his belongings spread out on the curb and a hastily scribbled "for sale" sign posted. After that, Clay just disappears. We replace him with a guy named Dave and continue playing ball.

Dave was driving down Sunset Boulevard with a friend when he saw a billboard featuring pasta vacuum and retired Dodgers manager Tommy Lasorda. It was at that moment that he realized just how much he loved the game of baseball. Raised by a single mom, he had taught himself to play with a broomstick in the alley behind their small home. He played ball in high school, and even when he was at the boys' home in Utah. He played while on the run in Alaska, and now that he was back home in Los Angeles and his life was finally on the upswing, he wanted to play again. His friend told him that he knew of a baseball team that needed a player, a team for guys just like him. He takes over at third base.

Two months later, Dave decides to relax with a little cocaine and heroin. It doesn't go so well. The next morning Mike L. stops by and finds him sitting in a chair, fully conscious and completely blue. One leg is folded behind him at an unnatural angle and his hearing is gone. It seems playing third base for the Pirates has become a real-life version of drumming for Spinal Tap.

"I threw him on my back and I took him down the stairs," Mike L. remembers. "While we're going down you could hear his foot hitting each stair—thump, thump—'cause it was just flopping around. He was taking a lot of deep breaths 'cause his lungs had filled up with fluid."

Mike burns rubber to County General. By the time Dave hits intensive care, his heart has stopped. The doctors manage to jolt it back into action.

"The doctor comes out and was telling me, basically, he won't live, and if he does, they're gonna have to amputate his leg. I went in and he had machines keeping him alive. A machine keeping him breathing, a machine working his kidneys."

Dave lingers in a coma for over a week with kidney failure. When he fades back into semiconsciousness, the doctors haul him into surgery to try to save his dying leg. But they've been giving him blood thinner to help his kidneys work, and when they open him up he begins to bleed to death.

At this point, the anesthesia starts to wear off and Dave finds himself able to eavesdrop on the doctors as they discuss his possible departure from the world. "I remember I think I'm on an operating table underneath the field at Dodger Stadium, and what they're saying basically is that if things get any worse they're gonna have to open the doors and I'm gonna have to be lifted up into the light. And I know that if that happens, I'm totally fucked."

Dave survives the surgery and the doctors salvage his leg. They say he'll walk again, but will have a serious limp and need a cane. So much for baseball.

***

Amidst all this, the team is actually starting to play better. Our obsessive tendencies drive us to spend endless hours at the local batting cages. Every Sunday we wash down handfuls of Tylenol and Motrin, soothing our wrecked bodies long enough to play some pretty decent ball. We're still losing games, but even those are close.

One day as we're warming up, Mike Coulter turns to throw the ball and we hear a cracking noise, like a tree branch snapping. Mike stumbles to the backstop fence and collapses. News from the hospital is shocking. The bone in his throwing arm has exploded into tiny fragments.

It's agonizing to see Mike, who found salvation in playing baseball again, and who started a team that has brought us all so much happiness, now unable to play, perhaps for a lifetime. He decides to stay on as manager, but you can see the heartbreak in his eyes every time he watches the rest of us take the field. I'm now starting to believe in a vengeful God, one bent on punishing us for our past junkie transgressions.

***

Then a crazy thing happens. We start to win more games than we lose. Heading into the final stretch, we find ourselves unexpectedly tied for first place with a team of cocky kids called the Blazers. Unlike us, they attract a large crowd of cheering family and friends. They also like to openly taunt opposing players. Mike Coulter tells me he thinks they take it all for granted—youth, baseball. Maybe he's right. I just remember the game when they heckled Masashi. How he seemed kind of perplexed and just kept pitching, too polite to respond.

The championship game is played at our home field in Griffith Park, and there are even a few locals there to cheer us on—a couple of tattooed girlfriends, Bob Forrest of Thelonious Monster, and some chain-smoking coffee addicts from the Café Tropical. As we prepare to take the field, I look over and see Dave standing on the grassy hill with a cane. He looks fragile, but it's great to see him. He waves hello and keeps his distance.

Standing in the outfield waiting for the first pitch, I find myself watching everything with an unfamiliar intensity. It's one of the few times in my life when I'm actually living each moment as it happens, like I can somehow grab hold of each second and inspect it before it passes me by. It's an unfamiliar sensation for someone who's made a career of checking out.

I gaze across the field at my teammates. Masashi's falling into a rhythm, throwing pitch after pitch to a crouched Dino. Jacob's at shortstop, wearing his dirty hat and staring ahead. Johnny's at third, shifting around and assessing the odds. Mike Coulter's in the dugout, arm in a sling, sharing a smoke with Chris. We look battered and bruised, like teams used to before the personal trainers, dietary supplements, and coke-dealer jewelry. And that's exactly what we play like—a real baseball team.

We play our best game ever that day, completely focused. This time it's not us that unravels with errors but the kids from Eagle Rock. Midway through the game Dave limps awkwardly down the hillside, enters the dugout, and sits down with the team. An inning or so later, he notices someone wearing his number, smiles, and tells him not to get too comfortable with it.

By the last inning, everyone's smiling and joking around. We know we're about to win, and it feels extraordinary. I suddenly have this image of Clay out there somewhere, alone. It makes me sad, not just for Clay, but for all my friends who didn't make it. Standing in the dugout with my baseball team, I wish they could all be there to feel what I'm feeling, and to know that it was actually worth it to grow up. And I want to make Keith Richards and Lou Reed run wind sprints up and down the field until they fall to their knees and beg for forgiveness.

The team clinches first place that day. A few weeks later, we all get shiny red plastic trophies. I haul mine out to my parents' house and stick it alongside my ancient Little League trophies.

***

A month later, I heard that Clay had resurfaced in a long-term recovery house. I went out to visit him and he looked thin and tired, like some old gold prospector found wandering the desert. When I told him the team won first place, he tried to smile. I asked him if he ever thought of us when he was out there on the streets and he nodded. "I used to think about the team all the time, actually. I would remember what my life was like, and it was always such a bright thought for me." He told me he'd stay in treatment for as long as it took, and who was I to argue? I put some money on his books —the petty cash account kept for him in the program office— hugged him and wished him luck. The next season Clay showed up on a pass from rehab and managed to squeeze in a few innings. Now he's working there and back on the team.

Dave started coming to the games in his old uniform, sitting in the dugout and keeping score. He eventually went in for a few innings at his old position. He still can't run, but when he does get a hit, the rules allow one of us to go in and run the bases for him. This isn't the big leagues.

Mike Coulter went back to Baltimore for surgery on his arm. After it healed the first time, the doctors told him it would be fine for "average" use. That didn't include throwing a baseball, so he had it rebroken and a steel plate inserted to make it stronger. He assures us he'll be back in the lineup a year from now, and if that's the case, we'll make a place for him. The team has kind of adopted the same rule as the mob: Once you're on the team you're never really off, no matter how far you stray, or how far life strays from you.

***

These days, whenever I'm flying in a plane, I look down and see the baseball diamonds. They look like nothing else, a brown square inside a larger green square, and they're everywhere. I imagine what it must be like to live in that particular town, to work there and feel like it's your home. And I think of how friends down there play baseball together on that very field.

I'm sure a lot of people think that grown men playing on an amateur baseball team, not to mention broken-down men fending off their personal demons, is slightly pathetic. But playing isn't about trying to recapture the past, not at all. It's about embracing the present. I've spent far too many hours regretting things I've done or fearing what lies ahead, and I don't think I'm so alone in this. But when I'm out there with my friends, playing ball, that all kind of disappears, and I find myself living every moment completely.

Last winter the Griffith Park Pirates played a night game. It was cold and windy and we were getting the shit kicked out of us by a bunch of old-school mustachioed jocks. In the last two innings, we started to mount a serious comeback. By the final inning, we were down by only one run with Little Alex (the count) on base. With one strike left in the game, and all hope nearly extinguished, Masashi pounded a ball into deep center field.

As Alex came across to score the tying run, the entire team piled out of the dugout and started screaming encouragement to Masashi, who was still tearing around the bases. Out in the field, some sheriff-type turned and rocketed the ball toward home. As Masashi touched third, the ball was already skidding across the infield toward the catcher's outstretched mitt. At the very last instant, Masashi leaped into the air and dove face-first across the plate, avoiding the catcher's tag and winning the game for us.

The whole team, including Clay and Dave, started jumping up and down like little kids, hugging Masashi, who was grinning beatifically through a mouthful of dirt. Everyone was laughing and smiling, Wally was joyously barking. And at that moment, nothing else in the world mattered. I was right where I wanted to be, playing baseball with my friends in Los Angeles.

Sons of the City

From the LA Weekly

The morning surf near Malibu has started to pick up, the waves appearing as dark lines against the still-overcast sky. The Red Hot Chili Peppers' bassist, Flea, seems almost giddy as he struggles into his wetsuit, grabs his board, and scampers down the hillside toward the water. He pauses on the sand for a minute of silent meditation, then throws his board into the water and begins to paddle out through the incoming breakers. Flea began surfing two years ago while visiting relatives in Australia, his birth country. Out in the lineup, he exhibits none of the natural hesitancy of a relative beginner. As sets roll in, Flea paddles furiously into each passing wave, occasionally tumbling headfirst over the falls with his board. When he finally does catch a wave, he lets out a series of joyful shrieks as he rockets down the face and carves out a respectable bottom turn before disappearing into an explosion of white foamy water. Paddling back out, he has a euphoric smile plastered across his face.

Onstage and in front of cameras, Flea exhibits a hyperactive confidence bordering on Tourette's syndrome. In person, he is energetic, yet thoughtful and almost shy. Preparing to eat a well-earned post-surf breakfast, he again pauses for a brief moment of silent meditation. Asked about it, he explains, "I was praying, I do it every day. I've never been religious, but I've always had a sense of spirituality. Rick Rubin turned me on to transcendental meditation about eight years ago, and it helps me to just be in the moment and not be scared of pain and anxiety or whatever." Flea goes on to tell how, after the enormous success of the record *BloodSugarSexMagik*, he completely fell apart both physically and emotionally.

In the wake of the 1991 CD's popularity, and with a young daughter onboard, he stopped doing drugs. But after an initial period of euphoria, he just collapsed. "I thought I was Superman, but it all caught up with me, and I just fell apart. I felt so sick. I was in bed all the time, and it was completely traumatic because I was so used to playing basketball all day and partying all night and rocking out. And then all of a sudden I couldn't do anything. I was embarrassed that I felt so bad. It was the first time I was really forced to look inward."

Flea looks around at the tranquil Malibu setting. "I was sort of wondering to myself. I live out here in Malibu now, am I going to get lazy because I'm kind of disconnected from the anxiety of the city? I've always had stress, and I grew up in L.A. and it made me who I am, and now I'm out here and I'm surfing, and it's just this relaxed lifestyle." He shrugs. "But then again, I know a week from now I'm gonna be out on tour slugging it out." Asked why he still does it, Flea replies, "More than anything, I have to say that I want to be of service to people. I mean, honestly, that's it. I think we're putting something beautiful out into the world that people can relate to. I feel like we're doing something real."

Nearly 20 years into the Chili Peppers' career, at a point when many of their contemporaries seem content to horde their shekels and recycle past glories, the Chili Peppers have produced, "By the Way." perhaps their boldest and greatest achievement yet. It is a diverse and complex pop masterwork that evokes Southern California, and particularly Los Angeles, as only a handful of previous records have done. So how did the band go from gyrating about with tube socks on their dicks and singing "I want to party on your pussy" to serving up one of the most accomplished pop records of recent times? Much like the aging Hollywood action star who has suddenly reinvented himself as a serious actor, the Chili Peppers have called upon their accumulated and tumultuous life experiences, added an almost obsessive willingness to push artistic boundaries, and taken a collective leap forward into the new. It feels less a calculated career move than a change borne out of sheer necessity, both musically and personally.

In the beginning, the Red Hot Chili Peppers were a joke—literally. What would later turn into two decades of success began as a one-off lark called Tony Flow and the Miraculously Majestic Masters of Mayhem. The four original band members, their brainpans soaked with LSD, marched single file across Melrose Avenue and took the stage of a small Hollywood nightclub. They went through some syncopated dance moves and then performed their only song, "Out in L.A.," with first-time performer Anthony Kiedis rapping about how exceedingly cool the four pals were. "People loved it," Flea recalls. "We didn't even know what we were doing, it just happened by its own force. We just started playing and it exploded. The music was unheard of. No one was doing anything like that." The band landed a record deal within a few months.

***

To understand how the Chili Peppers could generate such initial excitement with only a handful of songs, one must understand how entirely original they were at the time. In 1983, A Flock of Seagulls was on the radio, *Risky Business* was in theaters, punk rock was washed up and hard drugs were the new barometer of cool. Think Brett Easton Ellis' nihilistic teen melodrama *Less Than Zero* without so many bisexual rich people. In a world presently overrun by a never-ending pestilence of shirtless white rap rockers, it seems nearly impossible to imagine an earlier time, yet music in the '80s was mainly perpetrated by Englishmen who jerked about as if re-creating Monty Python's famous "Twit Contest." Sure, there was some ingenious dancing on the other side of the racial divide, Michael Jackson was still living here on planet Earth, and countless Jheri-curl-sporting Boogaloo Shrimp clones were spinning about on cardboard slabs, but the notion that hip, white musicians could actually groove and exhibit a sex appeal beyond cross-dressing and suicidal depression seemed unheard of at the time.

The Chili Peppers earned a reputation for outlandish mugging, alleged sexism, and onstage nudity in these early years. Flea believes this acting out cost them with music critics, especially in Los Angeles, where they have continued to receive little notice over the years. "I think it's because [the *L.A. Times'*] Robert Hilburn came to see us play at the Club Lingerie in 1983, and we said a bunch of really obnoxious stuff and he hated us. And because he hates us, it's like we don't exist. Twenty years of putting out records and living in Los Angeles and being a band that pours our heart into everything we do, and not a spot of ink."

On the radio a few months back, David Bowie stated that the American public really only remembers the three biggest things any artist has done. Sadly, for the Chili Peppers, this would consist of nudity, drug addiction, and funk rock. It is true that much of the public still envisions the band as the irreverent pranksters they once were, but, while capable of the occasional provocative outburst, the Chili Peppers have actually evolved over the last decade into rather serious artists. Rick Rubin, who has produced the band's last four records, theorizes, "Taking your clothes off is interesting; putting your clothes back on is less interesting. It's less noteworthy. They're kind of still in the putting-their-clothes-back-on phase. But there's no question that the quality of the work just keeps getting better and better. But the general public does still seem to view them as a party band."

One of the raps on Los Angeles is that the town is populated by beautiful people incapable of any deep intellectual thought. This is relatively the same logic that says all athletes (and especially surfers) are stupid, the premise being that you can either have a good body or a good brain, but not both. The accuracy of this equation can easily be disproved by simply noting the hordes of unsightly simpletons who roam the planet. Nevertheless, it is a trap that plagues even modern music, where to be taken seriously you can be pretty or strange, but rarely athletic-looking. The Chili Peppers have always flaunted their physicality, regularly performing shirtless with not a flabby party ball among them. Though fast approaching middle age, the band has unfortunately aged exceptionally well. This combined with a willingness to interject overtly sexual images into their lyrics has pretty much damned them to the populist mainstream regardless of how inventive their work is. Only the band's past appetite for heinous amounts of narcotics gets them slightly off the hook with arbiters of cool. Still, be so audacious as to mention their latest disc in the same category as a hallowed masterpiece like the Beach Boys' Pet Sounds, and you'll get laughed out of the used-record graphic-novel store. But the truth is, the Chili Peppers' latest release is one of the most interesting and creative new records around and arguably belongs in the pantheon of great Los Angeles albums with the works of the Beach Boys, the Doors, the Flesh-eaters, X and others.

John Frusciante is sitting half-submerged in the swimming pool of his Hollywood Hills home, the lilting psychedelia of Tyrannosaurus Rex traveling out from a stereo. If you've seen pictures of Frusciante from 10 years ago, his appearance is noticeably different. In youth, he was almost male-model pretty, posing for photographs with a confident smile bordering on a sneer. Nowadays, he appears somewhat fragile-looking, more disheveled artist than Southern California skate punk. He is surprisingly talkative, blending a sure intellect with slightly New Age spirituality, not particularly warm, but engaging. Frusciante was a teenage fan of the band when he was tapped as their fourth guitarist. "Everybody I ever met," he says, "I would tell them, 'The Chili Peppers are my favorite band, I love them.'"

***

He had migrated from the doldrums of the San Fernando Valley to study guitar at the Musicians Institute in Hollywood when drummer D.H. Peligro of the Dead Kennedys introduced him to Flea, and he was asked to join the band. Chili Pepper drummer Chad Smith shakes his head. "He was 18 when he joined the band. Eighteen! The first band he was ever in was his favorite band. It would be like me having joined fucking Led Zeppelin!"

Frusciante recorded two records with the Chili Peppers during his initial go-round, the second of those, *BloodSugarSexMagik*, being the album that launched them into mainstream stardom. This sudden ascent to mass popularity left the acutely sensitive Frusciante increasingly unhappy and disillusioned. "By the time we were recording on *BloodSugar*," he recalls, "it was very clear to me that I could make the world beautiful if I controlled my environment. But that if you rushed me into the middle of a traffic jam or put some ugly billboard in front of me, anything that wasn't pleasant to me, I had no idea how to protect myself against it." This discomfort also translated to fellow band members, whom he believed were too eager to sell themselves out for fame and fortune. "I felt like they thought to be successful they had to pretend to be something, to make funny faces and jump around and be silly and make weird jokes, because that's what was going to make them successful."

At the time, Frusciante felt the band should model themselves after underground heroes like Black Flag, the Velvet Underground and the Butthole Surfers, and not concern themselves with selling vast amounts of records. Accordingly, he began trying to subvert the process, refusing to do interviews and changing the way he played during their live shows. "He was almost like the fan in some ways," Smith says. "Like, 'I used to like them, but now everybody likes them, so I don't like them anymore.' But we didn't really change. It's just a mentality, that rebelling-against-being-popular thing. As soon as the record started to take off, he would just do the opposite of whatever he thought he was supposed to do. If it was time for a lead, he'd unplug his guitar. If it was time for a rhythm break, he'd just go completely off." On tour in Japan, Frusciante abruptly quit the band and flew home to Hollywood.

After leaving the Chili Peppers, Frusciante dedicated himself full-time to a bout of heroin addiction that left even the most jaded in Hollywood aghast. With infection spreading throughout his arms and teeth rotting out of his head, many assumed the end was looming. Yet somehow, he managed to linger in this isolated and somnambulistic state for six bleak years before finally being hospitalized. Drug-free and on the mend, Frusciante was eventually asked to rejoin the band. "He comes over to Flea's garage, and I didn't know what to think," Smith recalls. "But once we started playing, it was just kind of like putting on an old shoe. It just felt good."

His arms scarred from skin grafts and his grill replaced, Frusciante now seems finally at peace with the uncertainties that fueled his initial departure. Sitting on a couch surrounded by an enormous and eclectic record collection, Frusciante explains how he has finally come to accept life as a famous rock star. He tells of how, when all alone in the depths of his addiction, images he had of artists like Jean-Michael Basquiat, David Bowie, and Leonardo da Vinci kept him alive. "And it matters very little whether these people were in tune with me on some subconscious level or were pure fantasy," he says. "The fact is, they kept me alive and they made my life feel like it was worth living. They made me feel like I had a friend. And this time when I joined the band, I was so thankful for being kept alive all those years by my images of people, that I was just like, oh great, let's send out images to some other people. To me what's important is the image that some kid in Montana has of me. If I make that person feel good, if I mean something to that person, it's just as real or more real than what I actually am."

***

Frusciante now eats healthy, practices yoga, and plays or composes music nonstop, seeming to have transferred his addiction from narcotics to the creative process. "I'm not saying that I've done all this with a purpose in mind when I was just destroying myself," he says. "It took a lot of suffering and a lot of confusion and a lot of searching. But I feel like I've been doing a good job for the last four years. I came back with a completely fresh perspective. I wasn't drugged and I wasn't off balance. I was starting from a brand-new place, and there's a lot to be said for that. There have been other people who have gone away and then come back and seen the world or music from a brand-new perspective and then done the best stuff that they've ever done. Not only musicians, but also people like Mohammed and Buddha and Jesus Christ. They all led sort of normal lives, then disappeared for a while and then came back, and that's when they had all their fresh ideas and stuff that they're known for."

Before heading into the studio to record, "By the Way," Frusciante began studying different types of music, looking for tools to expand the band's sound. Spinning a rare EP by the Human League, he explains his recent fascination with '80s synth-pop stars. "I learned all Gary Numan's synthesizer parts on the guitar because that was very much in the way that I wanted my guitar playing to be. I was spending a lot of time learning parts from Kraftwerk and Depeche Mode, Human League and Orchestral Manoeuvres in the Dark, because I was finding that people who were programming synthesizers in this early electronic music were playing in a very minimal way, where every single note means something new and every note builds on what the last notes were doing."

That is not to say that, "By the Way," sounds like a new-wave dance club filled with clove cigarettes and geometric haircuts. Unlike, say, the Strokes, who seem to merely cut and paste their influences into vaguely new arrangements, Frusciante has glommed onto various techniques, then used them to create something fresh. There may be a cold and futuristic Gary Numan–like synth weaving through the song "Warm Tape," but it is placed between warm guitars and melodic harmonies. Much like contemporary hip-hop, the songs on the album seem a collage of existing, sometimes disparate influences in the service of something entirely new.

When Frusciante was still conflicted over his place in the pop mainstream, his friend Johnny Ramone revealed to him that for the entire time the Ramones were together, they had wanted to be like the Bay City Rollers. "And you know, when you see someone like him," Frusciante says, "You see that that's what was actually behind him… And you know, a lot of these great people like Lou Reed or the Germs, they would have loved to have been very successful.

"When I'm writing music," he continues, "I feel like I'm doing the same thing as the Ramones or the New York Dolls or what any of these people were doing, just writing music because you're excited. But I understand the level of success of the band that I'm in, and I'm not going to try to pretend that what I really want is to be smaller. I know what we're doing when we're going in there and putting the vocals under a microscope and making a verse shorter and a chorus bigger. I know what that's all about, and I'm not in any kind of fight with that. I see that the purpose is to make a pop record."

The band had initially recorded a batch of minimalist punk songs as a counterpoint to the more heavily produced tracks on the new record. Yet when they sat down with Rubin, whose judgment they have come to implicitly trust, he suggested they leave the punk songs out. To him, they lacked the uniqueness of the other compositions, and he thought the band should stick to what they do best. The band, including Frusciante, agreed. "People want to think that a fast drumbeat or loud guitars and a guy screaming makes it punk," Frusciante says, "but I know I'm making music with the same feeling that I was getting from those records. The energy of punk is so inside of me and it's so much what draws me to keep doing what I do, that it's in there inside the music, and when it doesn't have any obvious remnants, that makes the music all the more intriguing."

***

Their producer concurs. "I think for a band that's been making albums for a long time," Rubin says, "finding new ways to express themselves keeps it interesting. And on this album, there were lots of lush vocals and an orchestra, which we'd never used before, and that just took it a new way. Maybe the next album will be much more sparse. I don't know the direction it will go, but I know that evolution and change is a good thing."

There may well be a painting of an aging Anthony Kiedis hanging somewhere in his Hollywood home, because in person the singer betrays few outward signs of being 40 years old, let alone a longtime ex-heroin addict. Perhaps like the old Twilight Zone episode, he has purchased some additional years of youth from a gullible elevator attendant; or, judging from recent pictures, Keith Richards. At an age when many men have lost hair and added chins, Kiedis arrives for rehearsal on a sleek, new Vespa scooter, looking like an athletic man in his late 20s. Gone are the exaggerated mannerisms and anti-social mugging of years past, replaced instead by a quiet and seductive politeness. When he talks of the band's history, as well as his own life growing up in Hollywood as a terminally stoned child actor, it is with a sense of warm nostalgia. He appears to have few regrets, though there remains a deep sadness when he speaks about the overdose death of the band's original guitarist, Hillel Slovak.

It was this heartbreak that would inspire the band's first truly introspective song and signal a new attention to the craft of songwriting. While Slovak's death was the catalyst for the song "Knock Me Down," it was the band's new guitarist, Frusciante, who would help to channel Kiedis' grief. "Here's what John did, which had never been done for me before," Kiedis explains. "I had lyrics about the loss of Hillel, but all I had were lyrics, no melody. And I brought it to John and said, 'These are the lyrics, maybe we could turn it into something.' He looked at my words and said, 'Okay, I've been working on this thing that I think might go with this.' And he just started playing guitar and singing a melody for these words that had no melody. He's so knowledgeable about affecting melody in original ways, and what he started to bring was this idea of writing different kinds of songs."

What is perhaps the best song on the new album, or on any Chili Peppers album for that matter, is also inspired by a close friend's death. On, "Venice Queen," Kiedis sings about his beloved friend and mentor Gloria Scott, a gray-haired, ex-junkie drug counselor from Venice Beach who helped Kiedis and many of his friends battle their drug addictions. When it was discovered that Scott had lung cancer, the Chili Peppers held a benefit concert for her at the Hollywood Palladium. When her cancer became terminal, they rented her an expensive apartment overlooking the Pacific Ocean, where she eventually died.

The song begins with a tense guitar resembling Mike Oldfield's Tubular Bells Exorcist theme accompanied by a low Joy Division–like synthesizer fading in and out. Another guitar emits mournful notes as the bass and drums gradually build to a fast, nervous pace, with Kiedis singing: "Does it go from east to west/body free and a body less…" and "Dropping in coming through the mesh/checking in just to get blessed." A few minutes in, everything drops out, and a lone guitar begins to strum like Pete Townshend on "Pinball Wizard," the bass and drums quickly joining in. What had seemed the tension of illness and impending death becomes a bitter-sweet celebration of a life well spent as Kiedis sings: "We all want to tell her/tell her that we love her/Venice gets a queen/best I've ever seen/We all want to kiss her/tell her that we miss her." Soon

Frusciante's voice is harmonizing behind him, and the song has the exuberant, driving-up-the-California-coast feel of the Mamas and the Papas. What began as a moody meditation on mortality and loss grows into a heartfelt tribute. It is an incredibly effective song, musically striking and intensely emotional.

Flea says that before recording the album, he and Frusciante had listened a lot to the melancholy work of Joy Division. "Sad music is beautiful," he says. "A lot of the music we play is definitely born of sadness. I mean, it's a sad world that we live in. It's a sad and beautiful world is what I say."

The new album showcases Kiedis as a vastly improved vocalist. Still not blessed with enormous range, he has learned like other rock singers—Mick Jagger, Joe Strummer, Iggy Pop—to use interesting cadences and emotional delivery to surprising effect. "One thing I really can't stress enough about this record is Anthony's growth as a singer," Flea says. "We would start playing stuff on this record, and he would just start singing melodies that were incredible. And I think probably that has as much to do as anything with making it a great record. He's just continually shown growth, and on this record, he really took everything to the highest level."

***

Still, it is a topic Kiedis appears weary of. "People always bring it up, but I just don't think about it," he says. "I just sing whatever comes to me. Some days I feel like I can sing anything I want, and some days I can't sing shit. But I try not to think about it so much. I just close my eyes and sing whatever I can."

On early records, Kiedis' lyrics tended toward simple, almost adolescent-like rhymes of self-congratulatory boasting and lustful fantasy. Over the years, he has matured as a lyricist, his subject matter becoming increasingly observant and revealing, his wordplay skilled and inventive. In the song, "This Is the Place," Kiedis addresses the search for romance amid the debauchery of L.A. nightlife: "This is the place where all the devils plead/Their case to take from you what they need/Can I isolate your gene?/Can I kiss your dopamine/In a way I wonder if she's living in a magazine." Later in the song, he looks inward, contemplating the behaviors he might have inherited from his once hedonistic father: "I don't want to do it/like my daddy did/I don't want to give it to my baby's kid."

Rubin believes it is this more revealing subject matter that has inspired Kiedis' enhanced vocal delivery. "I always found Anthony's lyrics interesting," Rubin says, "but it seems like they have gone from interesting abstract lyrics to personal, heartfelt lyrics. And I think that's because he's not telling a sex story but conveying a real emotional experience. It's fueling the singing to be better and more emotional because the substance of it is coming from a deeper place in him.

"I would say Anthony has gotten more secure in who he is," Rubin continues. "He's always been fighting demons, but it seems like his relationship with the demons is better than it used to be. I don't know that he would ever say that he's cured, or the demons are gone. But it does seem like his relationship with the demons is a much more positive one. Does he feel like a happier person? That's not so clear."

Drummers in rock bands tend to either be out-of-control court jesters like Keith Moon, or anonymous and easily replaceable components like whoever played in all those other bands. In the Red Hot Chili Peppers, Chad Smith is neither. He provides both a steady backbeat and some much-needed stability. It seems no coincidence that the most down-to-earth member of the band is also the only one who didn't grow up in the self-obsession of Los Angeles.

Smith is from the suburbs of Detroit and has lived the rock & roll dream. A local hero back home, he was playing the bar-band circuit with no real prospects, besides drunken backslaps and the warm advances of countless wet T-shirt contest winners, when he packed up and headed for Hollywood. In town for just under a year, he landed an audition with the Chili Peppers. Sporting poofy Billy Squier hair, a tattered Guns N' Roses T-shirt, and some way-too-short cutoffs, Smith sat down and attacked the drums, oblivious to the attitude being thrown his way. The band loved it. "We were laughing so hard," Kiedis recalls, "We told him, 'Okay, shave your head and you're in the band.' He said, 'No,' and we thought that was even more punk than being pushed around by a bunch of assholes like us." Reminded of this, Smith offers, "I think I've just been sitting in for the last 13 years. They never actually said, 'You're in the band.'"

Along with Frusciante's new songwriting influence, it was Smith's hard-hitting drum style that initially broadened the band's appeal. The first Chili Peppers songs to receive mainstream radio play, "Knock Me Down," and "Higher Ground," both feature Smith and a percussive drumming that bordered on straight-ahead rock. "He came in and had a monstrous influence on our sound," Kiedis says. "We'd always had great drummers, but Chad's particular sound was something that was so solid and profound that it kind of spoke to the world. Cliff Martinez is the coolest drummer of all time, but his shit only spoke to a kind of more refined, intellectual art-funk vision of the world. We loved the hell out of his shit, but Chad's simple, powerful rhythms reached a lot more people."

***

As of late, Smith's drumming has become much more varied and subtle. No longer strictly in the John Bonham school of monolithic pounding, he has broadened his approach considerably, often employing several different beats and styles within the same song. On the album's title track, he works a driving neo-tribal beat similar to '80s postpunk sensations Bow Wow Wow, before returning to a more conventional kick, snare, high-hat for the silvery pop choruses. Like bass virtuoso Flea, who rarely employs his trademark funk-slap style on the new record, Smith is now strictly in service of the song. "You just have to do what you think fits," he says, "and the music that we're making now is more melodic, so we have a different role. I played with this blues guy in Chicago not long ago, who said, 'If I can hear you, you're playing too much.' And I knew exactly what he meant."

Smith has finished a barrage of interviews at the posh Chateau Marmont hotel and is dining in the celebrity-strung courtyard, looking surprisingly relaxed and unaffected. Upstairs on a nearby balcony, there's an intense glare of bright lights as Flea gives yet another interview to promote the band's upcoming tour. Several hours before, each new group of foreign reporters had asked Flea to do something outrageous and funny for the camera, and he is still visible up there, gamely, if not reluctantly, hamming it up.

It is perhaps telling that the songs for, "By the Way," were mostly written and recorded at a suite in the famed Chateau Marmont. It is an atmospheric, old Hollywood hideaway that has seen more than its share of high-end depravity. Comedian John Belushi died there shooting speedballs, Montgomery Clift recuperated there after his disfiguring car crash, and countless stars and starlets have shacked up in the bungalows. Columbia Pictures founder Harry Cohn was quoted as telling his two stars William Holden and Glenn Ford, "If you must get into trouble, do it at the Chateau Marmont." The hotel now uses the quote as an advertisement.

Like in the X song, "Sex and Dying in High Society," what makes Los Angeles such a fascinating artistic milieu is its abundance of contradictory images—violence amid opulence, poverty in a perfect climate, spirituality fueled by depravity, fame and crushing loneliness. While Kiedis claims to have never intentionally written a song about L.A., for him to address almost any aspect of his life is in many ways the very same thing. More than any current artist, Kiedis appears to have lived the quintessential L.A. experience, having been a child actor, a drug addict, a rock star, a hedonist, and a spiritualist. In simply observing the stations of his life, he delivers telling snapshots of the city.

With his face on MTV and countless magazine covers, Kiedis still rides through the streets of L.A. on his small scooter. And while he has witnessed the ruin of many friends, he still views the city as a forgiving and hospitable locale. "Los Angeles is a part of me," he says. "This is where I got turned on to the magic of life and music and sex and drugs and movies and all the friends that I'll be with for the rest of my life. These are the streets that I walk up and down and where I wrote my lyrics. It's where I got stabbed, it's where everything happened to me. So it's part of who I am, and I don't look at it as inhospitable because it never was. It's the greatest place in the world."

The band has arrived at a Hollywood soundstage to tape a segment for the venerable English television show Top of the Pops. An enthusiastic audience culled from their fan club has packed the room and is pressed excitedly against the stage. The Chili Peppers stroll out to ecstatic applause and, as cameras roll, launch into a symphonic, big-beat, glitter anthem called, "Don't Forget Me." Teenage girls elbow one another and stare lovingly up at Kiedis as he undulates before them, singing, "I'm the rainbow/in your jail cell/all the memories of/everything you've ever smelled." A bearded Rick Rubin stands back in the crowd, smiling and nodding his head to the music. Pausing before the next song, Frusciante casually removes his shirt, exposing his severely scarred arms. Audience members exchange concerned looks and whisper to one another, but Frusciante simply closes his eyes and starts to play his guitar. The song builds and he leans back on his heels, lost in the music. Afterward, the Chili Peppers are walking offstage when someone from the crowd hurls a single white tube sock. It lands directly in the band's path, yet none of them appear to see it.

***

In a current musical environment of near pedophilic youth obsession, a veteran band has sold an experimental pop record to the world. Glance at the stark portrait on the album sleeve and you can see the complete transformation. While years ago they would have mugged and posed for the camera, now they simply stare off, like somewhat shell-shocked survivors. What's on the surface seems so much less important, it's what's inside that matters. After 20 years of constant unraveling and rebuilding, the band has drawn from the experiences of a lifetime and made the album of their career.

"It feels like it's a new time," Kiedis offers. "No one feels like, oh well, we did some good stuff in the past. I mean, fuck all that. That was then… let's do something great today."

The Hep-C Generation

From Slake: Los Angeles

The bridge into Tijuana passes over a sea of cars before descending into the bustling chaos of a city in a near-celebratory act of self-destruction. In the past several years, Tijuana's violent narco wars have claimed the lives of three police chiefs and hundreds of civilians, including children. Severed heads have begun turning up around the city like some Aztec-inspired admonition. I walk past a pool of evaporating vomit on the ground and copper-colored smears on a graffiti-etched wall.

It's morning and the sun is already frying the pavement. Crossing the bridge with me are tired-looking Mexican families, sunburnt German tourists, and a handful of solitary men who I assume are seeking various forms of vice found far easier and cheaper amid the lawless poverty of Mexico.

I pass through a heavy iron turnstile and emerge into a bustling Tijuana plaza. The place is crowded and abuzz with commerce–taco vendors cook up an assortment of meats and cramped storefronts offer cheap souvenirs. Within seconds a taxi pulls to the curb.

"Adelitas?" the driver calls out through the open window, referring to one of the larger Tijuana brothels.

"No, *gracias*," I reply.

"Cheecago Club?" he counters, naming another.

I keep moving. After a few blocks, a small guy with a mustache confronts me. I notice that he has a fully formed hand sticking out of his shoulder where his right arm should be.

"Marijuana?" he asks in a high, raspy voice.

I shake my head. He falls in step alongside me. I can't tell if he's twelve or fifty.

"You want girl? Very young, has a tight pussy. Hundred dollars."

"No thanks."

"What you need, amigo? I get you anything you want."

"I'm just here to see a doctor," I say, and turn back toward the plaza, scanning the horizon for what the receptionist at the William Hitt Center described as a tall building with a red medical sign. On this morning I belong to another sect of frequent visitors– those in search of a miracle. This setting seems an unlikely place to find one, but they say the polluted waters of the River Ganges can heal as well.

My journey into Mexico that morning began almost three decades before in the backroom of a small record store on a boulevard in Pomona lined with Pentecostal churches and vacant lots. The town, thirty miles east of Los Angeles, was once the hub of a thriving citrus industry. It has long since degenerated into one more suburban slum. A gangly ex-radical in his thirties who had glommed on to the local teenage punk scene ran the store. He sold vinyl over the counter and purple tabs of LSD under it. His hippie friend, "Jesus," would drive an old ice-cream truck around the city selling weed and hallucinogens as well as the occasional snow cone. My friend Rozz had recently dropped out of high school and was living with his new boyfriend, Ron, in a back room of the store where the two of them explored sadomasochism. One would periodically hear the sound of a cracking whip followed by a delighted scream. Love was in the air.

They kept a dead cat in the freezer. Ron had brought in the somewhat flattened feline after it had been run over by a slow-moving parade of Chicano lowriders. One night, a biker girl from the neighborhood stumbled into the shop tripping hard on LSD. Someone opened the fridge and handed her the cat. She didn't even flinch, just smiled and began to stroke its icy fur. The cat was eventually defrosted and used in a particularly visceral art performance Rozz and Ron staged for a crowd of punks at a nearby gallery. The members of the fearsome band TSOL arrived that night carrying their homemade "art shields"—medieval-looking things made from cardboard that featured strategic slits through which the band could watch without being splattered with detritus from the "performance."

Next to Pomona is Claremont, where I grew up. With its tree-lined streets and eight private colleges, it resembled an idyllic East Coast college town inexplicably relocated to the sun-scorched suburbs. Toward the end of the seventies, my friends and I abruptly rejected the musty remnants of hippiedom and embraced the new punk culture coming out of England. We cut our hair short, wore thrift-store clothes, and adopted a demeanor of perpetual discontent. Before long, we stopped attending school and spent our days in unsupervised homes getting drunk, fighting, and listening to records instead. On weekends we would find someone older with a driver's license and head for Hollywood to see our favorite bands play.

I had heard of Ron nearly a year before any of us actually met him when, on a summer day, I was sitting in a van with some mustachioed Black Sabbath types mooching drugs. They mentioned Ron, saying he was "totally queer" but still pretty tough, and always had good pills. When Rozz and I encountered Ron in person, he was wearing tight pants and had strawberry-blonde disco hair. The three of us ended up at the local park, where Ron insisted that I chop off his hair with my mom's kitchen scissors. A week later, Rozz and I were in my parents' furnace-like garage rehearsing songs for what would eventually become our band, Christian Death, when we heard someone pounding on the door. We stepped outside to find Ron wearing a black trench coat, and, at the time when a man caught with even a single stud earring could evoke suspicion if not outright hostility, he had an assortment of large wooden crucifixes dangling from both ears. We were, needless to say, impressed.

The following months were an exhilarating but strange time. Everyone seemed in a hurry to grow up and move beyond the relative safety of our not-so-distant childhoods. People were exploring all sorts of exotic avenues musically, sexually, and chemically. My friend Dee, who as a black ex-skateboarder was already deemed a freak by society, took to dressing like a punk witch doctor in dark turtlenecks and bone necklaces. Under Ron's tutelage, Rozz evolved from an introverted punk with dandruff to an increasingly charismatic figure with his own cadre of oddball disciples. The rest of us traded in our leather jackets and Dead Kennedys records for dark suits and pointy Italian shoes. We started reading William S. Burroughs, J. G. Ballard, and Nietzche. But nothing proved more efficient at achieving that desperately desired separation from our parents' world than injecting a syringe of ghetto-bought heroin.

And so I found myself in the back room of the record store rolling up my sleeve and holding out my arm. I had just turned sixteen. Ron was next to me, cooking up a spoonful of Mexican heroin, steadying himself on a beam he had been using to suspend and whip a local skate punk who would eventually spend decades in San Quentin. The ominous sounds of Throbbing Gristle warbled on the stereo.

"Are you ready?" Ron asked in a surprisingly gentle voice.

I nodded and watched intently as he slid the needle beneath the skin of my arm. He located a vein, pulled the plunger back until it registered a cloud of blood, then shot the mixture into my body. Euphoric warmth engulfed me. For the first time in my life, I was exactly where I wanted to be. It was the beginning of a collective love affair that would very nearly destroy us all.

***

Hepatitis C is the most common blood-borne virus in the United States. An estimated 4.5 million Americans are infected, four times the number of those who are HIV positive. Most are current or former IV drug users, including some who used a syringe just once many years ago. The disease is most prevalent among people born between 1945 and 1965, most of whom became infected during the seventies and eighties. Many of these people have only recently found out they have the virus. Hep C is a hard disease to track; it can incubate for years, even decades before symptoms begin to show. A small percentage of those who contract hepatitis C clear it in the first few weeks. Usually, it progresses unnoticed until it's in the chronic stage. Chronic hepatitis C methodically attacks the liver and is the leading cause of cirrhosis and liver cancer. As a result, it is also the most common reason for liver transplants. It's estimated that 8,000 to 10,000 died from hepatitis C in the United States last year.

I have the virus. So do nearly all my old friends. My best friend from childhood, who I grew up skateboarding and smoking pot with, is infected. The pink-haired pixie from San Fernando Valley whom I took to my senior prom has it, as does the formerly homeless, nihilist friend with the cigarette burns on his arms who, as an adult, became a wealthy production designer on blockbuster films. In fact, the majority of the kids I knew in the thriving Los Angeles underground of the late seventies and early eighties–from the slam-dancing kids at the Starwood to the young junkies emulating Johnny Thunders outside the Cathay de Grande–have hep C.

Now, decades later, as so many of us are finally figuring out how to enjoy our lives, this unwanted remnant from the past keeps surfacing all over town like that half-forgotten friend just released from prison who now insists on hanging out and destroying everything.

I first discovered that I was infected with hepatitis C in the late eighties when Blue Cross denied my application for health insurance. When I asked why, I was told my blood tests revealed elevated liver enzymes. At the time, I was just relieved not to have HIV. Hep C was still relatively unknown outside of the medical community, and the diagnosis seemed meaningless. Years later, when I began suffering bouts of debilitating fatigue, I went to see a liver specialist. He informed me that the disease was steadily destroying my liver.

The good news was that it would take decades before I would develop cirrhosis or liver cancer. The bad news is that was twenty years ago.

After years of neglecting the diagnosis in favor of uneasy denial, I finally went to see a doctor. It had become increasingly hard to overlook the effect the virus was having on my life. Some days I'd be so tired it was all I could do to make it from my bed to the couch. As a result, I had become increasingly depressed. There is a psychologically corrosive effect to feeling bad all the time. I felt prematurely old, and the future seemed fraught with uncertainty.

I decided to look into interferon therapy in hopes of eradicating the virus from my body once and for all. Taking interferon is the only medically accepted treatment. It has a 50 percent success rate and comes with a host of unpleasant side effects, including suicidal depression, muscle aches, chronic fatigue, anemia, blindness, thyroid failure, and baldness. I figured with some antidepressants and a toupee I would be fine. A few days after going in for a consultation, I got a message from a doctor telling me to call her back as soon as possible. That's rarely a good sign. When I reached her, she told me the precautionary ultrasound revealed a centimeter-large "spot" on my liver.

"It's still in the early stages," she told me.

Early stages of *what*, I wondered after hanging up the phone.

I met with my doctor the following day. The hospital's liver department discussed my case and decided I should proceed with interferon treatment. At the same time, the doctors would try every method available to investigate the spot.

"But if it grows at all," she said. "We will have to act quickly."

***

Ron had been bugging me to do the interferon for at least a year before I finally gave in. He had recently completed the treatment, and it had been successful. The two of us both got off drugs in the mid-eighties. In my case, legal pressure from multiple theft charges forced me into a rigid custodial treatment center, where I remained for eighteen months. After graduating, I lived in a small apartment with some aging ex-cons before slowly transitioning back to a more creative existence. Ron had stopped drugs only to discover that he was HIV-positive. Back then, the diagnosis was an almost certain death sentence. Yet somehow Ron not only survived, he flourished. A performance art career begun with a flattened cat had morphed into something far more sophisticated, though no less provocative. He achieved worldwide acclaim and notoriety. At one point in the mid-nineties, arch-conservative Senator Jesse Helms propped up a large photo of a seminude Ron on the Senate floor and used him to rail against public arts funding.

And while the two of us managed to survive, many of our old group weren't so lucky. My friend Rozz achieved cult fame as a singer, but succumbed to addiction and depression and eventually hanged himself. Dee shot a man while robbing a bank for drug money. Facing life in prison, he tried to escape from jail by fashioning a rope from bed sheets and climbing out a window. The sheets were wet and he slipped, falling seven stories to the pavement below, where his girlfriend was dutifully waiting with a getaway car. Others had died far less dramatically, quietly overdosing alone after lives of crushing disappointment. Often, it seemed like those of us who lived were left with the virus as a reminder of a shared past that sometimes felt like the prologue to a tenuous future.

The night before injecting myself with the first shot of interferon, I call Ron. The irony of seeking support from the same person who first shot me up with heroin seems strangely perfect. He is brutally honest about what I will face.

"I think you really need to describe it to people as chemotherapy," he tells me. "You need to let people know you're going to be really sick and you might go a bit crazy."

Ron says that while doing the treatment he became so isolated and depressed that he lost many of his friends.

"I had a lot of these relationships where people called me 'Daddy' and they would do all their complaining to me. And I finally told them, 'We can't do this anymore.' I didn't want to hear it. I stopped answering the phone and returning calls."

After a few months, the drugs in his system made him feel radio-active.

"I was living out in the desert of Palm Springs. The only time I would leave the house would be to walk to the corner store wearing just my boxer shorts and flip-flops. My eyelashes got really dry and then one day they just fell away."

The following morning, I play my final game of baseball for the team of ex-junkies and punk rockers I've been playing with for years, the subject of my book *Wrecking Crew*. I hit a looping single and jog up the baseline. The first baseman, a grizzled ex-minor leaguer, gazes out at the outfield grass.

"It sure is a beautiful day, isn't it?" he says.

"It really is," I reply.

That night, I go into the bathroom with a small vial of interferon and a syringe. The treatment involves taking pills daily and injecting liquid interferon into the stomach or leg muscles three times a week. I slide the syringe into my thigh and push the plunger. Some old Pavlovian reflex has me expecting a euphoric rush, but I feel only a dull ache at the injection site. I take some Tylenol and go to sleep. The following morning, I wake up with what feels like the flu. The second day, I start to feel somewhat radioactive, but it isn't bad, just different. As the week progresses, my muscles begin to ache. I have a constant headache and my mouth is dry. I lay out on a slab of sun-heated concrete for hours with my little dog, Wally, sleeping next to me.

Two weeks later, I'm sitting on the couch watching baseball and fighting back tears. Everything has started to make me cry. The only two emotions I can access are intense melancholy and near-homicidal rage. Social invitations have tapered off. The already-strained relationship with my wife is at a breaking point. And then one night, Wally stands and begins to stagger across the floor toward me. She tumbles over and begins to violently shake. Foam comes out of her mouth. I have no idea what is happening and begin to panic. Is it a stroke? I pick up her limp body and carry her to my car.

The following afternoon, Wally is given an MRI and then diagnosed with a brain tumor. She comes home drugged on antiseizure meds. I sleep restlessly on the couch that night, twitchy from my own drug cocktail and traumatized by what I have seen. I keep waking up and looking over at Wally. She seems equally unsettled, peering through the darkness back at me.

When word gets out that I am doing the treatment, it seems like everyone I know has questions. Most want to know if the side effects are as bad as they have heard. Some of my male friends considering the treatment ask if I am losing my hair. A female fashion designer with the virus wants to know if the drug caused me to lose weight. When I tell her it has, she giddily says she might do it after all. Many have been trying "alternative" therapies.

I have lunch with a writer friend and listen as he describes the variety of New Age treatments he has tried: a special sauna installed in his house at the suggestion of one enterprising doctor, an intravenous vitamin C drip that another physician administered at substantial cost. When he begins talking of some healer in San Francisco who can tell when someone last had sex by merely passing her hands over them, I feel a little lost.

I try to hide my skepticism, but my doubts about such treatments seem to put me in the distinct minority among my peers with the virus. Friends who once railed against the silliness of New Age hippies are now ingesting expensive Chinese herbs sold by bearded shaman types, doing acupuncture religiously, drinking expensive holistic potions, and sipping tea doused with homeopathic remedies sold by an aging fashion model. One friend informs me of her plan to fly to Russia for an experimental "stem cell" treatment. When I go online to check the clinic's Website, I become convinced she will spend her remaining years as an unwilling organ donor for cologne-soaked black marketeers. It all reminds me of how sad I felt upon hearing how the supremely cool and confident Steve McQueen spent his last months in Mexico receiving coffee enema treatments for his cancer. The live-fast, die-young bravado of youth inevitably disappears and then one night you're lying awake staring into the darkness, gripped by the realization that you're far closer to the end than the beginning. And at that point, you just want more.

***

The waiting room of the William Hitt Center in Tijuana is decorated with plastic plants and feels like an oven. None of the people sitting there appear to be Mexican. We exchange awkward smiles. A woman in a Bob Dylan T-shirt has circles under her eyes and has lost most of her hair. The receptionist apologizes for the heat and says the air conditioner is broken. I remain standing and survey the framed medical certificates on the wall. I do this in every waiting room or office I enter. The offspring of two college professors, I am, by default, something of an academic snob. The certificates on display here are from institutions I have never heard of. They also look photocopied. I remind myself to be open-minded.

Dr. Hitt greets me with a smile and a handshake. He is tall, in his seventies, has snowy white hair, and looks remarkably like Sydney Greenstreet from *The Maltese Falcon*. Hitt escorts me around the clinic, passing through a room where several patients recline in plastic chairs with tubes running from their arms to suspended bags of blood. He motions to a container of yellow liquid and tells me that besides the ozone treatments, his clinic offers something called "urine therapy."

Hitt leads me into a converted supply closet cluttered with an assortment of medical supplies. There are some syringes and a bag of blood on the counter. He gestures to the wall and something that looks remarkably like a fuse box with the word "ozone" hand-painted on it.

"*That* is our precious ozone machine," he says with a smile.

I first heard about ozone therapy as a treatment for hep C when several members of a hugely successful Los Angeles band started doing it. Though not close friends, they are part of the extended L.A. punk/ex-junkie fraternity, most of whom carry the virus. In the early eighties, we had all frequented the same nightclubs and injected the same drugs in the same bathrooms, sometimes with the same syringes.

Not long after that, I was sitting at Dodger Stadium with another friend from the old days. Chris was one of the seminal, and sometimes violent, Huntington Beach punks who left an indelible mark–slam dancing, buzz cuts, gang fights–on West Coast youth culture. Now he resembles Buddha, if the rotund deity were outfitted head to toe in blue Dodgers regalia. The conversation, as it usually does, eventually turns to our worsening livers. I was surprised when he informed me that his fatigue had all but disappeared and his tests were apparently improving. He said he had recently started therapy, which I assumed meant interferon. It didn't. Like others, he had gone to Tijuana for the ozone treatments.

Hitt leads me to his office. It is cluttered with magazines and photocopied pamphlets. On his desk is a small microscope of the sort one might use in high school science class. I inform him that I have hepatitis C and am interested in how ozone treats the virus. He hands me some photocopied articles and launches into a spirited sales pitch, punctuated with all sorts of numbers and statistics. When I mention that I am on interferon, he immediately criticizes the treatment.

"As you probably know," he says somberly, "approximately three out of 100 die from the drug itself."

This alarms me. Not because I fear for my well-being, but because it seems so obviously untrue. That would mean for every 100,000 people treated with the drug, 3,000 would simply drop dead. No matter how paranoid one might be about so-called "big pharma," no medical treatment that wasn't supervised by Josef Mengele could get away with that high of a mortality rate.

Hitt's theory is that introducing ozonated blood into a person will eradicate all the viruses in his or her body, making hepatitis C a nonfactor. He says that, unlike most physicians, he doesn't use blood tests to verify success but instead examines nasal Pap smears under his microscope.

"I'm interested in looking in that microscope and seeing the total amount of viruses a person has," Hitt explains gesturing to the microscope on his desk. "And if I can bring their viral population down, then I can keep that person pretty darn safe."

He fails to mention that one can't actually *see* viruses with a regular microscope like his. To do so Hitt would need an expensive electron microscope about the size of his desk.

Just then another doctor leans in, apologizing for the interruption.

"Don't mean to bother you," he says to Hitt. "But I'm looking for a slide. I think it's a send-in."

"Yes, right," Hitt says thoughtfully. "Could it be in the box?"

"You know, I don't know. It *could* be in the box."

With that Hitt reaches for a box on his desk and pulls the top off. Glass slides of nasal smears tumble out onto the floor. Both doctors bend over and begin picking them up. The other doctor eventually stands, holding a patient's slide between his fingers. He smiles at me.

"Found it."

The episode reminds me of that scene in the Marx Brothers film *A Day at the Races* where Groucho (aka Dr. Hackenbush), Harpo, and Chico pretend to be doctors.

After his colleague leaves, I ask Hitt about his medical background. He tells me he isn't actually a medical doctor but has PhDs in immuneology and microbiology. His medical degree is honorary, awarded to him by a Mexican medical school.

"The university president gave me one so I could lecture there," he admits with a shrug. "But at the highest levels, I give lectures. I'm a member of the Mexican Psychiatric Association, the American Psychiatric Association, and the Canadian Psychiatric Association– because of the work I've done in drugs."

Back home in Los Angeles, I do some research. I discover that in the eighties, at the height of the AIDS crisis, Hitt was sued by the state of Texas for fraudulent practices and for making false claims about his qualifications. He was prohibited from representing himself as a doctor.

Later, I speak on the phone with a Dr. Robert Baratz from the National Council Against Health Fraud. He systematically debunks Hitt's ozone therapy, saying, among other things, that the premise of our bodies being loaded with viruses is just not true.

"The body is *not* loaded with viruses," he explains. "Our body has something called the immune system and T-cells, which kill viruses. Sure, some viruses, like HIV, can hide inside cells so they can't be killed by our immune system. But since the ozone isn't getting inside the cells, it can't kill those viruses either."

I ask him about many of the alternative remedies my friends are trying. For each one, he explains the fundamental flaws.

In the end, he tells me, "Look, 'alternative medicine' is really a misnomer because it is not an alternative to medicine. It's a marketing tool. A true alternative is a scenario where you can take United Airlines or American Airlines, but you'll get there either way. The more accurate term for all this is just quackery. They're pumping these people full of hope and telling them they will feel better and so some of them do, which is a placebo effect. Until you do a clinical test, you can't claim anything."

***

The following week, as my forty-first birthday nears, I'm in the basement of a hospital in Hollywood. A half-hour before, a technician removed some of my blood, mixed it with radioactive material, and injected it back into my body. Now I'm lying on my back and a large box is circling my body like a hyper-inquisitive robot. The department is called nuclear medicine and the doctors are using the procedure in an attempt to see the spot on my liver. When they're done, the technician tells me that when I piss I should flush the toilet several times and wash my hands thoroughly.

That night, I make the mistake of going online and reading all about liver cancer. I almost throw up. Death is common. A survival of five years is considered success. Because I was raised by godless intellectuals, there is no heaven waiting. Death simply means nothingness forever. As a child, my mother tried to soothe my anxiety by explaining that we live on in the memories of those who love us. It didn't work.

My doctor calls the next morning and tells me to come in. When I arrive, she isn't smiling and looks tired. We have become friendly over the last few months and her demeanor alarms me. She informs me that the spot has grown.

"I was upset by this news," she says. "But then I was thinking about it, and there *is* hope. We have caught this early, which makes a difference."

I understand what she is saying, but I feel nothing. It's as if the whole thing is happening to someone else on a TV show I am watching from my couch. She says I have an appointment with a surgeon in two hours.

I call my brother and ask him to meet me at the surgeon's office. He has always been more pragmatic than me, and I have come to rely on him in situations such as this. The surgeon is a tanned man in his late sixties with a reassuring confidence. He wants to go in and cut out the part of my liver with the spot. The other option is to wait and see what happens.

"What would you suggest if I were a member of your family?" I ask. It's a question I had always planned on using if faced with a moment like this.

"It's a safe operation," he says matter-of-factly.

I look over at my brother who nods.

"Let's do it," I tell the surgeon.

The surgeon reaches for a leather day planner and lazily flips through the pages. There is something comforting about him scheduling my operation around golf games.

"How about tomorrow afternoon?" he asks.

"Too soon," I respond.

"Okay, how about in two weeks then?"

"Sure."

***

I'm driving through the vast, sprawling Los Angeles Harbor district to meet an old friend. His name is Manny and he works as a longshoreman. He used to be a punk rocker. I park my car near a huge, gray cargo ship. Manny eventually arrives at a small doughnut shop situated near the docks. He's an enormous Hispanic biker with a black beard, slicked-back hair, and heavy boots. I have come here because Manny is the only person I know who has had a liver transplant. As strange as it once seemed, it's now something I might have to confront.

A few years back, Manny's liver began to shut down because of hepatitis C. He began pissing and vomiting blood and his legs became swollen. Manny's doctors immediately put him on the list for a new liver. After waiting for more than a year, the call finally came.

"I was bringing the trash in and my wife came out and said, 'Your liver's ready.' I just waved and told her I would be right in. I thought she said, 'Your dinner is ready.' When she told me I was suddenly scared."

I ask him what the surgery was like. I have never had any kind of operation, and the thought of going under terrifies me.

"It was supposed to be a five-hour operation, but it lasted thirteen because my liver was so swollen," he says. "I wake up and there are tubes in me and I was hallucinating. I gained 110 pounds from all the liquids. My nuts were swollen up like baseballs."

Manny tells me he went home after two weeks.

"They said I wouldn't work for a year. But I went back to work in a couple of months. They said I wouldn't drive, but I started riding my motorcycle pretty soon after that."

He tells me that as bad as the surgery was, the prospect of not getting a liver had been far more frightening.

"I've known people who are thinking of getting them on the black market now, they're so desperate," he says.

Unfortunately, the virus is still in Manny's system and is now attacking his new liver, a common occurrence. As a result, he must go back on interferon. We sit there for a while talking about old times and old friends.

"Punk rock came and my life changed," he says. "It was a scene where anybody could do anything. Those nights in Hollywood were some of the best times of my life."

As the conversation continues, it seems like so many of our old compatriots from that period are now dead. We do a casual count and come up with more than twenty names. Most of those who survived now have hep C.

***

The night before my surgery, I make the mistake of once again going online. This time my research involves the unnerving phenomenon of people waking up during the operation. The first account I read is of a woman who regained consciousness during an operation that involved removing one of her eyes. Turns out the procedure requires a lot more "torque" than one might imagine. The woman won a lawsuit but remains understandably traumatized. This pretty much sets the tone for the night. By the time I'm done viewing a documentary on people committing suicide by jumping off the Golden Gate Bridge, the alarm goes off and it's time to go.

The surgery is merely an absence of time. I hear later that after making a long incision in my stomach, the doctors removed my organs and placed them in a bowl resting on my chest. At that point, the surgeon carved off a chunk of my liver, and then everything was replaced and the incision stapled shut. The real fun begins afterward.

At some point, they tell me that I don't have cancer. It's a testament to the sheer agony I am in that I couldn't care less. I stay in the hospital for five days. The cancer ward is not a particularly joyful place. There are screams and the sound of people crying. My roommate is an older Chinese man with lung cancer. The nurses encourage the two of us to fart, which in any other situation would make me happy. It's harder than you might think with one's organs still resettling. When I finally manage a short, tuba-like burst, my Chinese friend applauds enthusiastically. Later, I pass a mirror and notice that my beard has turned white.

It takes months to recover. The incision gets infected and I have to stuff the wound with gauze every few hours. It's one of the most painful sensations I've experienced. At one point, I am shuffling around with a pink discharge dripping from the open cut in my stomach when my friend "Pig," a hulking ex-con with survivalist tendencies, walks in. He immediately goes to his jalopy pickup truck, retrieves a medical kit, and proceeds to expertly clean and bandage my wound. He does it several more times in the following weeks. Where and why he learned to dress gaping gut wounds is something best left a mystery.

The interferon treatment lasts eighteen months. During this time, I experience a parade of physical and psychological side effects. For a while, I'm covered with a violent red rash. I suffer from blinding headaches and near-crippling fatigue. There is a constant sensation of heat emanating from within my body and my mouth is perpetually dry, the inside of it covered with sores. But it is by far the psychological effects that prove the most insidious.

I gradually fall into a depression like nothing I have ever experienced. I almost stop working altogether. The most I can muster is an occasional record review. I give the new album by aging hair band Whitesnake a rave suitable for *Sgt. Pepper's*. I also start to obsess on things and spend hours watching online videos of European football hooligans rioting. Soon, I am reading hooligan message boards and conversing with them in English slang. At my worst, I attempt to arrange a massive battle between two rival English hooligan gangs. The plan fails when I am discovered as an imposter. I begin watching reality television relentlessly and weep during episodes of *Star Trek*. My only joy comes from attending Dodgers games.

For the entire time I am on the treatment my blood tests show that the virus has disappeared. A month after finishing, it comes back. Everything that happened–the surgery, the interferon–was of no real physical benefit. Besides the ten-inch scar across my stomach, the experience left me with little more than a sustained depression and some sort of consolation from knowing I tried. One morning, I try to think of something, anything really, that would make me happy. Nothing comes to mind. I eventually start taking antidepressants, but by then my marriage is over and I am virtually homeless, living on a friend's couch.

My dog, Wally, continues to have seizures, but thanks to medication she is still alive today. So are many of my old friends. We still discuss our livers at Dodgers games and while hiking through the hills above Hollywood. For the most part, I just try to focus on enjoying the individual moments of my life. Some days I'm so fatigued, I sleep up to 20 hours and still wake up tired. Other days, I feel relatively normal. Years ago, when I was a nihilistic teenage junkie, I never imagined I would live to see anything even resembling middle age. Back then the idea didn't appeal to me in the slightest. Now I want more life. My doctor recently informed me there is a new interferon treatment on the horizon that promises to be more effective with fewer side effects. I'll probably give it a shot.

A Perfect Game

Excerpt from Wrecking Crew, The Really Bad News Griffith Park Pirates

The championship game was played on our home field, in Griffith Park. It was, of course, a beautiful, clear morning. As I walked down into the dugout, I was surprised to see Mike Coulter sitting on the bench with his arm in a big plaster cast, looking slightly deranged from the painkillers. He was sucking on a cigarette and hunched over the team's roster, looking like Orioles skipper Earl Weaver if he was decades younger and had spent his adolescence on drugs listening to the Dead Kennedys. Mike glanced up at me and barked, "Batting seventh, right field," then returned to his brainstorming session.

Johnny was at the far end of the bench, sitting upright and staringly unblinkingly at the empty field before him.

"How's it going, Johnny?" I asked, studying him as I set my equipment down.

"I'm good. Ready to play," he responded, still without blinking.

I started to warm up, throwing the ball back and forth with murderer Don. I glanced around at my teammates. Jacob was wearing a filthy uniform, and with his braces and strange hairdo, he looked like a mental patient. Will and Mike L. were standing together, and Mike L. had taken his shirt off so he could display a brand-new tattoo of a swashbuckling pirate that covered his entire rib cage. The two were listening as Dino regaled them with another of his delightfully depraved exploits, this one having something to do with a prostitute's well-worn shoe. The once-reserved Masashi was standing with them, laughing and looking unshaven and a bit hung over.

"Nooo… You really did that?" I heard Masashi ask.

"You would have sniffed it, too, you little Jap bastard," Dino replied. "I went to Japan with my friend's band, and you fuckers sell girls' panties in fucking candy machines, so I know how perverted you people are."

Masashi nodded enthusiastically. "Yes, I know."

By the time the game was about to start, I was pleased to see that we actually had a small cheering section for the very first time. Sitting in our section of the bleachers was a motley gathering of Pirates supporters from the neighborhood, tattooed girls and guys who all looked a little unnatural in the early morning sun. Among them was a man in a Panama hat and white linen named Bob, who was the singer of a long-standing L.A. band called Thelonius Monster. Chris's roommate, Hurricane, was there as well. He was now well-aware of his old friend's cross-dressing tendencies and, much like the rest of us, had shrugged it off as no big deal.

The team huddled together in the dugout. Mike stood up on the bench and delivered an impassioned (and somewhat incoherent) inspirational speech that ended with the rather touching message: "Try not to fuck this up. Now come on and let's beat these dirty motherfuckers!" On that tearful note, we clasped hands, shouted "Pirates!," and sprinted onto the field to a smattering of applause and sarcastic comments.

The team definitely looked battered and bruised that day, much like the baseball teams you see in old black-and-white photos and news-reels from years ago, before all the million-dollar contracts, personal trainers, and coke-dealer jewelry. And that's exactly what we felt like that day—a real baseball team. As I jogged out into right field, I noticed a gaunt figure on the hillside, half obscured by the sunlight. I could see that he was leaning on a cane, and as I got closer, I knew it was Dave, or perhaps his ghost. I waved to him, and he raised up his hand in a sort of salute.

Standing there in the outfield waiting for the first pitch, I found myself watching everything with an unfamiliar intensity. It was one of the few times in my life when I was actually living each moment as it happened, like I could somehow grab hold of each second and inspect it before it passed me by. It was an unfamiliar sensation for someone who has spent his whole life checking out. We played our best game ever that Sunday, remaining completely focused. This time, it wasn't us who unraveled with errors, but the cocky kids in the opposing dugout. If we played them in a seven-game series, like in the big leagues, then I'm pretty sure we would have lost. But for one single game, we were able to give it our all, and that was enough. Right off, we jumped to an early lead, and then we just kept hitting lots of hard grounders and line drives, followed by the occasional long bomb pounded by either Chris or Mike L. The mood in the dugout during those first few innings was guardedly optimistic. We'd lost way too many early leads to feel anything close to confident.

Midway through the second inning, Mike L. and Johnny walked up the hill and invited Dave Huffman to come and sit with us. He limped awkwardly on his cane down the hillside, looking slightly embarrassed, then entered the dugout and sat on the bench with the team. At some point, he noticed Don wearing his old number, smiled, and told him not to get too used to it.

Masashi pitched a great game for six innings and then started to wear down. Mike Coulter decided to send him back in for one more inning, and as we took the field, I passed Masashi standing atop the mound. He called over to me, "Johnny boy!"

I walked over. He smiled and said, "This time, don't say you still love me even if I lose, okay?"

I nodded. “Masashi, if you blow this fucking lead, I will hate you until the day I die.”

He nodded and touched my shoulder with his glove. “Okay, thank you.”

Acknowledgements

Thanks to all the enablers of John's writing: Janet Duckworth, who saw in "Hardball" what would become *Wrecking Crew*; Laurie Ochoa, who can see an ace all the way up a sleeve; publishers Sean Manning, Tyson Cornell, and others I'm sorry I'm forgetting; and, of course to Arty Nelson, who introduced me to John when John was taking his first stabs at making sense of all this. Thanks, too, to John's family and friends for putting up with his shit (Jesse!) and taking me in. And to Deedee for giving him, and us, Ravi. And, of course, big hugs to Iris Berry and Punk Hostage Press for the enduring friendship, collaborations and for always knowing what's up.

–Joe

About the Author

John Albert grew up in Southern California. As a rebellious teenager in the late 70s. He co-founded the influential Goth-punk band Christian Death. He was drafted into drumming for Bad Religion for a time, and, in typical fashion, taught himself to drum. After a court-mandated rehab stint, Albert found success as a writer focusing on the rough edges of life in his beloved Los Angeles. Albert contributed feature articles and essays to numerous regional and national publications as well as literary journals and anthologies. He frequently wrote about the lives of his hard-bitten and hilarious cohorts. “Hardball” for the *LA Weekly*, earned Best of the West Journalism's Best Sports Writing Award in 2000 and developed into the critically acclaimed memoir *Wrecking Crew.*

John passed on May 3, 2023.

More Books on Punk Hostage Press

Danny Baker
Fractured – 2012

A Razor
Better Than a Gun in A Knife Fight – 2012, *Drawn Blood: Collected Works From D.B.P.LTD., 1985-1995* – 2012, *Beaten Up Beaten Down* – 2012, *Small Catastrophes in A Big World – 2012, Half-Century Status* – 2013, *Days of Xmas Poems* – 2014, *Puro Purismo* – 2021

Iris Berry
The Daughters of Bastards – 2012
!=All That Shines Under the Hollywood Sign – 2019
The Trouble with Palm Trees – 2021
Gas Station Etiquette – 2022

Yvonne De la Vega
Tomorrow, Yvonne - Poetry & Prose for Suicidal Egoists – 2012

Carolyn Srygley-Moore
Miracles Of the Blog: A Series – 2012

Rich Ferguson
8th & Agony – 2012

Jack Grisham
Untamed – 2013
Code Blue: A Love Story ~ Limited Edition – 2014 – Paperback – 2020
Pulse of the World. Arthur Chance, Punk Rock Detective – 2022

Dennis Cruz
Moth Wing Tea – 2013
The Beast Is We – 2018

Frank Reardon
Blood Music – 2013

Pleasant Gehman
Showgirl Confidential – 2013
Rock 'N' Roll Witch: A Memoir of Sex Magick, Drugs, And Rock 'N' Roll – 2022

Hollie Hardy
How To Take a Bullet and Other Survival Poems – 2014

SB Stokes
History Of Broken Love Things – 2014

Michele McDannold
Stealing The Midnight from A Handful of Days – 2014

Joel Landmine
Yeah, Well... – 2014
Things Change – 2022

More Books on Punk Hostage Press

S.A. Griffin
Dreams Gone Mad with Hope – 2014
Pandemic Soul Music – 2022

Nadia Bruce-Rawlings
Scars – 2014
Driving in The Rain – 2020

Lee Quarnstrom
WHEN I WAS A DYNAMITER, Or, how a Nice Catholic Boy Became a Merry Prankster, a Pornographer, and a Bridegroom Seven Times – 2014

Alexandra Naughton
I Will Always Be Your Whore/Love Songs for Billy Corgan – 2014
You Could Never Objectify Me More Than I've Already Objectified Myself – 2015

Maisha Z Johnson
No Parachutes to Carry Me Home – 2015

Michael Marcus
#1 Son and Other Stories – 2017

Danny Garcia
LOOKING FOR JOHNNY, The Legend of Johnny Thunders – 2018

William S. Hayes
Burden of Concrete – 2020

Todd Moore
Dillinger's Thompson – 2020

Dan Denton
$100-A-Week Motel – 2021

Jack Henry
Driving W/ Crazy, living with madness – 2021

Joe Donnelly
So Cal: Dispatches from the End of The World – 2022

Patrick O'Neil
Anarchy at The Circle K – On the Road with Dead Kennedys, TSOL, Flipper, Subhumans and... Heroin – 2022

Richard Modiano
The Forbidden Lunchbox – 2022

Shawna Kenney
I Was A Teenage Dominatrix 3rd Edition – 2023

O.R.
Ophelia Rising – 2023

Mike Roche
I Play With Giants – 2024

Made in the USA
Columbia, SC
19 June 2024